What people are saying about...

JUBILEE

"My friend Amanda is inspiring, but her most attractive trait is her love and devotion to Jesus! This 40-day devotional will take you deeper into a love and understanding of a good, good God who is always with us, always for us, and always transforming us. Get ready to fall deeper in love with God and find hope in both the ordinary and extraordinary days!"

-**Ann Wilson**, Cohost, Family Life Today; author, *Vertical Marriage* and *No Perfect Parents*

"Every day life is loaded with opportunities for reflection. Amanda gently invites you into hers, reflections that will deepen, expand, and challenge you. Amanda trusted God with 40 days of her life (and shared it with us). Will you trust God with your next 40 days? This book can help."

-**Ron Deal**, Family trainer, therapist, and bestselling author of *Building Love Together in Blended Families (with Dr. Gary Chapman)* and *The Smart Stepfamily*

"In Jubilee, Amanda takes us on a beautiful journey towards healing, faith and wholeness. Her authenticity is often raw and introspective as she explores the deficits in her own faith walk and invites the reader to grow with her in the goodness of God. As you embark on this forty day devotional, the end result will be inner transformation and knowing Jesus in a more intimate way. That should be the goal for every believer. Thank you, Amanda, for your obedience and openness to lead others into God's love and healing."

-**Jane Hamon**, Senior Leader: Vision Church @ Christian International, Author: *Dreams and Visions, Discernment, Declarations for Breakthrough, The Deborah Company, The Cyrus Decree* and *Confronting the Thief*

"Amanda's words speak into the heart of every woman who earnestly seeks God. In her honest conversations with the Lord, we see evidence of the Holy Spirit's work of intercession, comfort, and guidance leading to renewed peace and steadfast trust. She shares her healing journey authentically with a rawness that draws the reader in with each read. I walked away knowing that I myself could use more time with Jesus and an excitement for what that would bring. One of my favorite statements she wrote was, 'imperfect is beautiful.' Such a powerful statement I now declare every time the devil whispers in my ear."

–**Misty Parenzan**, Author, *He Was Always There*

"You can only give away what you have first received. Amanda's journey to freedom becomes your own as she masterfully weaves together her story to take us on a journey of full redemption with Jesus. At times, we make following Jesus all about what we do instead of who we become. This devotional will help you become and walk in the fullness of who you were created to be. There is no greater gift."

–**Cody and Jenna Wilson**, Founders and Pastors of Living Army

"Jubilee is a beautifully written devotional of allowing God to Father you in all places of your life journey. If you want to grow in relationship with Jesus and experience His heart healing, this devotional is for you. As we read through Amanda's daily journey, we found ourselves reflecting on our own relationship with the Father/Jesus and His faithfulness to us and we began to be washed in His words of love and affirmation over us. We personally loved the prompting to pause/reflect and invite the Lord to speak and define our vision of who He is as our loving Father.

Thank you for trusting the Lord, Amanda and responding to His prompting to publish this devotional!"

–**Brady and Olivia Gardner**, Co-Founders and Pastors of Living Army

"In my twenty-one years of learning and knowing my Savior Jesus, I have seen that nothing will ever fulfill or satisfy like time spent in God's word and in His presence. Those two things are THE bridge to true freedom. In a transparent way, Amanda invites you to experience the same kind of freedom she has found. Her zeal for the Lord is evident in the 40 entries she has penned."

—**Autumn Miles**, CEO, Author, Host of The Autumn Miles Show

JUBILEE

FREEDOM AWAITS ON THE OTHER SIDE OF HEALING

A FORTY DAY DEVOTIONAL

AMANDA ARMSEY

ABOUT THE AUTHOR

Amanda is called "Mama" by two beautiful daughters, and if you ask her, she will say she is raising warriors. She calls Metro Detroit, Michigan "home," but her heart is sprinkled all over the world from years of travel, living abroad, and mission work.

After building a career in Dual Language Immersion education, the Lord plucked Amanda out of traditional schooling and brought her home. This replanting opened the door for her to pursue her ultimate loves - writing, relationship, and ministry - and came with the fulfillment of a pipe dream: homeschooling her daughters in their second language, Spanish. When she isn't homeschooling or doing all the mom things, you can find her somewhere outdoors, buried in a book, filling journals, adventuring with friends, or in the kitchen. She is passionate about people, has a heart for women, and spends more time laughing than anything else.

Amanda is passionate about doing life with her girls, so where she is, they usually are, too. From hikes to street evangelism to bike rides to serving the homeless, the three of them live on mission for Jesus and love every second of it. She is determined to cultivate radical boldness in her daughters, which means living with abandon herself. In their down time, they enjoy having dance parties, cooking and baking, bike riding, snuggling up on the couch with a book, and having their weekly "girls' nights."

DEDICATION

Aside from everyone who helped make this possible, this is dedicated to anyone who has ever been where I was when I sat down to write it: lost, confused, and feeling a combination of helplessness and hopelessness. That place is not your destiny.

And, to my daughters, who not only saved me from the Amanda I once was, but who also lead me into the arms of Jesus daily by simply existing. You bring clarity to my confusion, empower me, and are my beacons of hope. May you always live a life of Jubilee. I love and adore each of you endlessly.

INTRODUCTION

Have you ever had one of those moments where you suddenly realize you're in a place you never expected to be? A place that feels unpleasantly familiar yet is so unrecognizable you have no idea how you got there? I have. More often than I care to admit, actually. The end of 2022's summer was one of those times.

For months prior to the close of that summer, I thought I was on the right path. In fact, I'd argue that I was. But then a string of events triggered past trauma, ignited feelings of worthlessness and rejection, and amplified the voice of self-doubt within me. I began to question every step I had taken up to that point, and with each question, peace dissipated. Something was severely off in my Spirit, but the immobilizing noise in my mind prevented me from figuring out what it was. Night after night, I found myself lying atop the rug in my office, crying until I had nothing left. I felt alone, afraid, and overwhelmed. I knew there was something I needed to see, but I didn't know how to see it.

My persistent visits to that rug seemed to pay off when God began to repeatedly present me with something: the number forty. He had my attention. A number representative of transformation, trial, and preparation, I prayerfully considered - and ultimately committed to - what I felt He was asking me to do: write for forty days. With no other instruction or perimeters for this commitment, I clenched the sliver of hope His request provided while questions reeled in my mind: How will I know what to write about? Why does God want me to do this? What is He going to show me? How painful is this going to be? What will be the outcome? The unknown made my Type A flesh twitch, but I knew His voice was calling me, and so I answered. The result of my answer is before your eyes.

A lover and proponent of authenticity, I wanted to preserve the rawness of my journey, which includes allowing you, my friend, to see the shallowness of my relationship with God at the beginning, its progression as I walked with Him, and my repeated visits to the same themes as He worked to shatter my unbelief, deepen my understanding of His Fatherly love, gain my trust, and, ultimately, lead me out of captivity and into His freedom - His Jubilee. The cry of my heart and reason behind sharing my wobbly steps toward Jubilee is that you would know you are not alone. There is no shame in being wherever you find yourself, nor in the process of moving forth - imperfect is beautiful, and it is what Jesus loves best.

Each day of this devotional contains a snippet of my

journey, corresponding Scripture, and a brief prompt, all intended to encourage self-reflection and entice conversation with Jesus. While most of the words you will read here are my own, the Words that ultimately matter belong to Jesus. I encourage you to not only open the Bible and meditate on His Word, but to seek His voice in prayer. He has so much He wants to tell you. And write...please write. Your words hold so much power and serve as a testimony of His goodness on your own journey to Jubilee.

As you embark, I leave you with encouragement I learned along my trek with Him: bare everything before Him. He is safe, He is kind, and He wants and has the very best for you. I am praying for you, that you would invite the Holy Spirit all the way in, so He may gently peel back the layers that have restricted the Father's love. For it is in that love that we find true Jubilee.

Bless you, sweet friend!

Amanda ♡

STUCK

And we know that in all things God works for the good of those who love Him. Who have been called according to His purpose
Romans 8:28

The first day of a new adventure brings with it a range of emotions. This one, however, seemed to arrive empty-handed. Or maybe it didn't. Maybe I am choosing apathy. Maybe I am choosing to ignore, to be blind, or to turn away. (It certainly wouldn't be the first day for that.)

The truth is that I have absolutely no idea what these forty days will bring. I wish I could say I am full of expectation, but with disharmony dancing in my mind, I am unable to have clarity of heart. I know I am not alone. I know I have never been alone. I know, both in mind and heart, that God chose me, created me, and has a purpose for me. Great purpose. I also know that I am my own greatest obstacle, complicating things with my emotions, desires, and fears.

I spent quite a bit of time today reflecting on God's will and what exactly that means. Certainly, He doesn't wish for us to experience agony, to make decisions that go against what He has for us, or to suffer at the hand of another person. Yet He allows those things to take place. And that is where I get stuck.

When I make a decision that goes against what He would have me do - be it my disobedience of what is clear in His Word or my negligence in seeking His guidance - and He allows me to walk the consequences of that choice, are the consequences His will? If yes, are they His sovereign will because He chooses whether or not to allow those consequences to come about, or are they His permissive will because He allowed me to sin and subsequently allowed the consequences to follow?

Amidst contemplating this, the Truth woven through the words of Romans 8:28 lead me to a place of rest, as I know that God uses all things - my sin and its ugly consequences included - for good.

Day one brought much more than I anticipated.

DAILY REFLECTION

In retrospect, I see instance after instance of Romans 8:28 playing out in my life - the increase in faith and trust brought through my daughter's congenital heart defect, the financial provision brought through a lengthy, exhausting fight for justice, and the deep intimacy and vast freedom that came after I claimed my worth and left a dark, unhealthy relationship.

Take a few moments to pause and reflect on the major events of your life - in particular, the struggles. Where do you see God flipping the script and turning things for your good and His glory? Using the struggle to grow and mold you? Where do you see His provision? His protection? Take a moment to acknowledge His goodness, and then, ask Him what He wants you to know about Him through this reflection.

DAY TWO
GUILTY BY ASSOCIATION

*Enter through the narrow gate because the wide gate and the broad
path is the way that leads to destruction - nearly everyone chooses
that crowded road! The narrow gate and the difficult way lead to
eternal life - so few even find it!*
Matthew 7:13-14 (TPT)

Pockets of day two contained another swirl of questions, found to be mostly rooted in one: Why am I even questioning what is and is not God's will? To put it plainly, it is because I am questioning His character. If I truly believed He is good, patient, kind, loving, gracious, generous, forgiving, and all of the other wonderful traits I have read and personally experienced, I would not be questioning His character or His will.

Recently, my daughters and I talked about Eve questioning God's character when she was tempted by the enemy in the Garden of Eden. The serpent's question conceived doubt in Eve's mind about what God had said to her, and his further questioning extended doubt's territory until it reached God's character.

Satan is no different now than he was then and I am no different than Eve. It is because of the enemy's manifestation through the flesh of countless people in my life that I have allowed my view of who God is to be tainted. I took the damage and heartache caused by destructive relationships, abuse, and abandonment and cast the blame for all of it onto my Heavenly Father. I know His thoughts and ways are higher than mine, and I know that if this is true about me, it is true about each of the people who have deeply wounded me. Yet, despite knowing His thoughts and ways are higher than theirs, I put God in the same category as them. I don't trust that He has my best interests in mind or great plans for me because those I have mistakenly trusted revealed their intention was to harm rather than prosper me.

It is easy to do that. When a dear friend seems to use our vulnerabilities to harm us, it is easy to believe God is just like them. When a marriage ends because of abuse, it is easy to believe God, who allowed the abuse to take place, is just like them. It is easy to view heartache as yet another instance of pain than it is to fight the pain with faith that my God is different, that He is better. It is easy to choose the path that requires no faith, no refinement, and no adjusting of myself

6

or how I respond.

But I'm not on that path. I, a Daughter of the King whose character I am questioning, didn't and don't choose that path. I chose the narrow path, and in choosing it, I must continually choose to hold tight to the heart of God. Otherwise, the enemy's continual efforts to morph my perspective of Him will weaken my faith and birth unbelief. And eventually, the pain that the lies cultivate will override everything, and I will be right where Eve was: choosing my will over His.

DAILY REFLECTION

We all have heard the term "guilty by association." While we would never want this to be applied to us, we readily project our perspectives of one person onto another. It takes work to unearth the truth beneath our emotion: that ultimately, we are dissatisfied with God. Recall a time when you have been hurt, betrayed, or offended by someone, reflect on what happened. Dig beyond the first layer until you uncover the disappointment you feel toward God. What do you wish He had done differently? Surrender it to Him as you walk in the realization of yesterday: that He flips the script and uses all things to work for His good.

DAY THREE
UNNECESSARY CHAOS

For God is not a God of disorder but a God of peace.
1 Corinthians 14:33a

A few blocks away from where I stayed with my host family in Buenos Aires, Argentina sits the widest avenue in the world: Avenida 9 de Julio. Countless times during my months of studying there, I crossed its sixteen lanes on foot. An incredibly wide thoroughfare, it was utterly chaotic. Apart from the traffic, there were people performing or begging for money at traffic lights, pedestrians were everywhere, and road rage was alive and well, to say the least.

A few blocks away from where I currently live is a trail that spans several cities. Winding through both wooded and residential areas, it provides respite in the midst of the busyness we live in. At some points, it is too slender to run or bike beside another person; overgrown foliage, the banks of a river, and steep drop-offs present dangers that require keen focus.

The keen focus required on la Avenida is different. Its spaciousness offers an elusive freedom, demanding that I pay attention to everything happening around me. There are a multitude of distractions, dangers, and other people to consider. On the trail, I need only be concerned with my next step. There are no distractions, dangers, or crowds that require me to re-route. The trail is far quieter and filled with unmatchable peace.

At one point in my life, I certainly considered la Avenida to be the choice path. Symbolic of the thrills of the world, living an Avenida life captivated me. I enjoyed being at the center of the hype - involved in everything and with everyone. In recent years, however, the trail life has become far more attractive - less noise, less people, less distractions, more solitude, more silence, and more peace. The seclusion I once revolted against has now become a source of life.

The narrow path is certainly my preference, but I live in a disorderly and, at times, lawless world. The question is: How do I walk in unmatchable peace in the midst of sheer pandemonium?

DAILY REFLECTION

Fairly regularly, I ask God to show me what is causing unnecessary chaos in my life. I ask, 'What am I carrying that isn't mine to carry? What am I focusing on that isn't mine to focus on?' As He brings those things to mind, I write them down. From there, I am better able to turn away from things that would otherwise distract me and lean into those He has called me to. Ask God to reveal to you what He has given you to steward so you can make your own list. If it helps, write a couple of practical steps you can take to help live a trail life in the middle of la Avenida.

THE "HOW," NOT THE "WHO"

Therefore, if anyone is in Christ, the new creation has come: the old is gone, the new is here!
2 Corinthians 5:17

An interesting thing about the sidewalks in Buenos Aires is that, oftentimes, they are tiled. (Yes, as in tile that we Americans would put in our bathrooms or kitchens.) The majority of the tile in my neighborhood was high gloss. More often than not, I would have to walk incredibly fast across that tile to reach any given destination because, in pure Amanda fashion, I was running late.

My last-minute nature became especially problematic on rainy days. High gloss tile gets incredibly slippery when wet. Slippery tile and rushing feet are NOT a good combination. Countless times, I slid into people, storefronts, or puddles. I am fully confident that no one witnessing my rainy day rush would have described me as graceful - silently frantic would have been more accurate. Frantic because my thoroughfare was essentially a Slip-N-Slide and I was in a rush, and silent because there was no reason to say anything. My words wouldn't stop the rain, nor would they change the material underneath my feet, nor turn back the clock. Neither would they remove any of the always-present obstacles along my route: the contents of the sheer pandemonium. I still had to navigate that.

Despite not living in the capital city of Argentina, having a vehicle to get me to where I need to go, and being fifteen years older, the path I take is still littered with chaos and, at times, brings less than pleasurable things that cause me to lose my footing a bit...despite the fact that there's no tangible slick tile beneath my feet.

Fifteen years later and living in the suburbs of a U.S. city, I no longer have to contend with slippery sidewalks and pedestrian-filled thoroughfares. Yet despite now using a car to get around, I still find myself rushing and facing chaos. It causes me to lose my footing a bit, just like in Buenos Aires. While I would still classify myself as frantic when rushing and silent when my voice won't change anything, there is one thing that is different about who I am today than who I was then: Jesus.

It is because of Jesus that I continue forth even after I lose my footing. It is because of Him that I can (most of the time) focus on my destination instead of what the path looks like. It is because of Him that I walk in unmatchable peace in the midst of sheer pandemonium.

DAILY REFLECTION

Paul's conversion is a clear example of what happens when we allow Jesus to have all of us. Jesus didn't change who Paul was, but how he was. Make a list of your core personality traits and gifts. In light of these, spend time pondering the difference in your life on both sides of Jesus. What did you worry about then that you no longer look twice at? How did you cope with things before Him compared to how you cope now? Acknowledge your growth, praise Him for it, and know that even when you lose your footing, His peace still reigns.

DAY FIVE

WHEN ALONG CAME A SERPENT

Be alert and of sober mind. Your enemy the devil prowls around like a roaring lion looking for someone to devour. Resist him, standing firm in the faith, because you know that the family of believers throughout the world is undergoing the same kind of sufferings.
1 Peter 5:8-9

Next to rainstorms, glossy tiled sidewalks, and rushing, my least favorite combination of circumstances involves incredibly hot and humid weather and the woods, because along with those come swarms of flying insects. Naturally, that would be exactly where God would call me to be so I could spend some time with Him today.

Looking back, my experience in the woods this afternoon bears more in common with my experiences with slippery tile and crossing incredibly wide avenues than one would think at first glance. It was near impossible to focus on where the trail was taking me while swatting away bugs, trying to be mindful of puddles, mud pits, fallen trees, and exposed roots, and attempting to wipe away the drips of sweat from my brow before they fell into my eyes. My physical surroundings barely qualified as a distraction - the cyclone of thoughts reeling in my mind held that prize. I hiked with a vengeance, frustrated that I was experiencing a swirling frenzy of thoughts instead of the very thing I came for: a taste of His peace.

In the last loop of the nearly five-mile trail, I finally surrendered my mind and began to pray, asking God to speak. Almost immediately, He reminded me of something that has surfaced frequently in my life over the last few weeks: the narrow path. Usually when He does this, I praise Him and acknowledge what He has brought to mind, and seek more of it. This was no different. Until it was.

Immediately after I began to zero in on Him, a snake slithered right in front of my toes, startling me. My heart raced and I thanked all of Heaven I didn't step on him, taking deep breaths to return to my previous level of zen. I left my angst behind me and on my tenth step post-unexpected encounter, the revelation hit:

I was in the very place God called me to be in that moment doing precisely what He had asked me to do when along came a serpent. The snake's presence startled me, jolted my thoughts away from Jesus, stopped me dead in my tracks, and required me to breathe and calm down – something that is not required of me in the presence of the Lord – before proceeding.

My confidence returned with each literal and figurative step that I took into this revelation. I resolved to turn back to photograph the snake, wanting to preserve the words of my revelation with a visual. But when my eyes landed on the place of meeting, the snake was nowhere to be found. I stood silently as my disappointment collided with God's voice: "What are you doing? You were going the way you were supposed to be going. You were doing what you were supposed to be doing. The enemy came and distracted you, and you turned around and went to go find him!"

He didn't need to say anything else. He was right. And so with one last deep breath, I did an about-face and returned to the Way, leaving the fear the enemy taunted me with in my wake.

I allow this to happen sometimes. I take my eyes away from where they should be fixed and allow my heart to be distracted by the smoke and mirrors the enemy famously uses to deter me. If I am not careful, if I do not turn back to Jesus and seek Him, I will not only remain distracted but I will also obstruct God's grace and His ability to heal me from whatever it was that the enemy threw at me.

In this case, fear.

DAILY REFLECTION

The enemy customizes his smoke and mirror charade for each of us. How does he distract you? My reaction to his attempts was to initially give him attention. Do you choose the same? Do you flee? Does he stain your thoughts?

After reflecting on those questions, write about a time you did an about-face when taunted and tempted by the enemy. If you can't recall such a time, write about an instance where the enemy was effective in his attempts. We all have them, and I have found great value in reflecting on such instances to see where I tripped up and what to do differently next time. Regardless of the route you take in your writing, you are victorious because you are here.

I stood silently as my disappointment collided with God's voice.

"What are you doing? You were going the way you were supposed to be going. You were doing what you were supposed to be doing. The enemy came and distracted you and you turned around and went to go find him."

DAY SIX

REJECTING HIM

Here I am! I stand at the door and knock. If anyone hears my voice and opens the door, I will come in and eat with that person, and they with me.
Revelation 3:20

I returned to what I'm going to call the Way again this evening. Those woods have become my escape over the last two years; a place where I don't have to be or do anything for anyone else. I never know what I will encounter - what God will reveal - when I am there.

At what I consider to be the top of the trail, there is a picnic table. On the rare occasion I bring my daughters with me, we always stop there to rest halfway through our hike. When I am alone, I slow my pace to take in the wildflowers surrounding it, but I never stop. My mindset is fixed on pushing forth, on seeking what is ahead.

Frequently when that picnic table enters my line of vision, the words of the twenty-third Psalm run through my head. Today, specific words within it echoed as I contemplated who Jesus, the Holy Spirit, and God are to me: "You prepare a table before me in the presence of my enemies." As He often does, He wove His Word with my contemplation, eventually speaking the same thing to me three different times, from three different perspectives: "I have prepared a table for us. Would you sit with me? Would you spend time with me there?"

Once, twice, I responded the same, not necessarily with words but with emotion. I felt giddy at the thought of sitting across from Jesus, my Ishi, to study Him and speak with Him. I was enthralled to simply consider what it would be like to spend time that way with the Spirit that lives inside of me. Yet when God asked, I just couldn't say yes.

My eyes welled with tears, but not because of guilt, condemnation, or anger. I cried because I was overwhelmed with sadness that I could decline an invitation from my Heavenly Father. I cried because I felt such elation about spending time with His Son and His Spirit, but merely considering sitting with God constructed a barrier I could quite literally feel in my soul. I cried because I knew the invitation included a journey to a new depth of healing – a depth that would require me to walk very difficult and painful things – and I just couldn't bear the thought of that.

And so, I didn't say yes; I said I was sorry. I said that I just couldn't do it. I turned my eyes back to the trail and I pressed on, and He remained there, at the door of my heart, waiting patiently for me to welcome Him in.

DAILY REFLECTION

All of us have experienced rejection of some kind. Recalling a time you were rejected, what did you feel and experience both during and as a result of that rejection? God is omniscient, which means He knows we will reject Him before He asks us to join Him, yet He still invites us. How do you feel knowing He adores you so much that He willingly endures your rejection and still finds joy in asking again? What might your lived experience be if you accepted - or even extended - more invitations, be them with God or with others?

WHEN I'M GOOD AND READY

Be dressed and ready for service and keep your lamps burning.
Luke 12:35a

One of my favorite stories to tell people is about the day I was born. I'm a firm believer that a person's birth story provides great insight into how they will be as a person. My oldest daughter was born on her due date and is as easy, organized, and predictable as they come. My youngest daughter was four days late, came at high speed and without any indication that she was on her way. She is a force to be reckoned with, to put it mildly, and runs at full speed into everything.

My birthday is August 19, 1986. Doctors back in the 80s let expectant mothers go much farther past their due dates than they do now. How far beyond, you ask? In the case of my mother's pregnancy with me, eighteen days. I camped out for almost three additional weeks until I was ready to make my debut, finishing off my extended stay with a standoff that left my mom in the car in the hospital's parking lot, anxiously waiting for the show to begin so she could be admitted. I came when I was ready to, and over 36 years later, I still don't typically do things until I am ready to. Including accepting God's invitations.

Historically, I elect to either not RSVP at all or to come right out and tell Him, "No, thanks. I just can't." There are certainly many reasons I could offer for declining His invitation to sit with Him. Each of those reasons is rooted in not being ready, but just writing that brings conviction. But the God of Noah, the God of Abraham, the God of Moses, the God of Jacob, the God of David, does not invite His beloved children into things that they are prepared for by their own accord. Rather, He invites them into things that require risk, that require courage, that require vulnerability, and that require them to ask Him to do what He needs to do.

Not being ready is the reason I didn't sit at the picnic table with Him, and so long as I allow my "unreadiness" to drive my choices, it will be the reason I continue to postpone the surrender of my mess, and, subsequently, to postpone His turning it into beauty.

DAILY REFLECTION

Have you ever expected to be ready for something only to be slapped with the reality that you weren't? Were you humbled by this experience? Did you see yourself differently afterward?

As I mentioned, God invites us into things that require risk, courage, vulnerability, and that require us to ask Him to do what He needs to do. What have you been avoiding or denying because you believe you aren't ready? What are you fearing - the process, the outcome, something else? What do you need to ask Him to help you do?

Not being ready is the reason I didn't sit at the picnic table with Him, and it will be the reason I continue to prevent a mess from being made into beauty, so long as I allow my "unreadiness" to drive my choices.

TUNNEL VISION

All Scripture is God-breathed and is useful for teaching, rebuking, correcting, and training in righteousness, so that the servant of God may be thoroughly equipped for every good work.
2 Timothy 3:16-17

Most days, I am on a mission. With two young daughters, a demanding career in education, a house to care for, and persistently attempting to care for myself, I best accomplish things with efficiency. This manifests in many ways, one being that my hiking boots find their home in my car during the spring and fall. In the name of preparation, I keep them there because a good rain in the months surrounding summer transforms my beloved trail into one big mud pie. Having them with me removes one step of preparation: my feet are equipped for wherever they may venture.

I was so deep in mission mode today that I parked at

the trailhead, jumped out, and headed in without a single thought. On the stretch through the field just before the trail, a heart-shaped leaf caught my eye. Upon stopping to admire it, I realized I was still wearing my running shoes. I was so focused on accomplishing all the things that I had forgotten to change into my hiking boots. An about-face and fifty steps brought me to my vehicle, I swapped out my shoes and returned to the mission.

Fifty steps later, I met the same leaf. Much like the first time, my view of it included my feet. I froze as I processed several thoughts, ultimately arriving at a realization: much like I need to be properly equipped to hike a muddy trail in the woods, I need to be properly equipped to walk where God calls me to walk. But being properly equipped requires preparation, which requires presence. In my case, being on a mission has formerly meant not being fully present. Much like I was hyper-focused on getting to the trail today, I have allowed my focus on the next item on my to-do list to hinder me from being fully present to the things that arrive that are on written on that list, which, a lot of times, are more important than the ones I list myself.

No more.

If I am not fully present because I am stuck on auto-pilot, I cannot be fully aware of my surroundings, which include the blessings and the attacks. If I am not fully present, I am unable to hear His voice, see through His eyes, and act as He asks. Simply put: if I am not fully present, I am not as effective as I can be because I leave no room for God. The only way for me to be fully present is to be fully prepared, which requires every bit of Truth packed in 2 Timothy 3:16-17. My preparation - my equipping - consists of immersing myself in His Word day in and day out. No exceptions, no modifications, no excuses. Because without His Word, how can I begin to recognize what I am not seeing, what I need to pay attention to, and which areas I need to grow in?

DAILY REFLECTION

Auto-pilot is a means of survival for some (guilty!) and life can be incredibly distracting. Do you tend to live systemically, focusing on what needs to get done or are you more of a go-with-the-flow person? How can God refine your norm to honor and experience Him in a fresh way?

BACKWARD

Lord, you are my God;
I will exalt you and praise your name,
for in perfect faithfulness you have done wonderful things,
things planned long ago.
Isaiah 25:1

Today felt different. Backward, even. I headed up my beloved trail knowing that something was going to happen; having already committed my heart to accept His invitation to the table, I was expecting that He was going to do something.

I am both a creature of habit and rule follower, which at Bald Mountain translates to always taking my trail the same way; at the first and second forks, I head to the right every single time. This time, I stopped at the first fork. Not wanting to take a single step outside of what God had for me, I considered turning left and taking the trail backward. I contemplated whether this was my idea or God's for a couple of minutes before He confirmed by sending a slew of birds off in that direction, and I set out on the trail backward.

With a tendency to allow my emotions to raise my expectations, I breathed deeply when I eventually arrived and sat at the table. I closed my eyes, laid my forearms atop it, my palms facing the sky, and told Him, "I'm here. I'm ready for whatever you have." I must confess that at that moment, my expectations rose. I think I was hoping for Him to just lay it out for me - to immediately tell me what it was in my heart that was an obstacle.

But He was silent. I waited, inhaling deeply and letting go of anything presumptuous with each exhale. He remained silent. My ears turned toward what was surrounding me. Crickets, birds, squirrels, chipmunks, and the wind all had something to say, their voices weaving into a beautiful symphony, Creation's symphony. I basked in it for a moment before His voice pierced its beauty. It was gentle, full of joy, dripping with love as He spoke: "Do you hear them, Amanda? They worship me with their song. All of them worship me and sing of my Glory. Their worship is a response. With their song, they are telling me, 'I love you, too, God,' because I first love them. Will you respond to my love?"

I stood, wondering how I could respond to a love I reject. It took a minute to remember I was taking the trail backward. Once I began to walk, my mind became fixated on that word: backward. I had been spending so much time thinking about all the ways various people had failed to care for me, projecting those negative circumstances, situations, and traits onto God. I had to do things backward in my mind just as I had with my feet that day. He was calling me to think backward, to allow my mind to be flooded with all the ways He is good instead of the ways they have not been.

DAILY REFLECTION

We are called to worship, which is more than just singing praise songs - it is a response to God's love that quite literally consists of every choice we make. How do you worship Him? In what ways are you choosing not to worship Him? Don't settle for your usual way of reflecting - think backward!

DAY TEN

BLESSINGS FROM REBELLION

You intended to harm me, but God intended it for good to accomplish what is now being done, the saving of many lives.
Genesis 50:20

It requires great effort for me to live out the faith that the promise in Romans 8:28 calls me to. I know that God really does work all things - bad included - for good, but I have to consciously work at allowing that knowledge to manifest in my thoughts, words, and actions, because, well, it is backward. Unless I am on the other side of the good God has made from something evil, it can be hard to picture something beautiful emerging from it. Ten days into this journey, I am not on the other side, which means I am in that gray area. I don't like gray areas. God knows that, which is why - through a trip to the bookstore today - He brought to mind a recent conversation that showcased His beauty-from-ashes nature gloriously.

En route to the bookstore, I was put in mind of a night at church several weeks back. I was partnered with someone I had never met before for a prayer exercise. The exercise consisted of asking God what He wanted the other person to know, and after my partner prayed and asked Him, she listed off three traits I possess – self-sufficiency, endurance, and stamina. She then recounted detailed experiences from my life (that she would have no way of knowing herself), connecting them to the cultivation of those traits. In doing so, she revealed something I had never considered before: the qualities – good qualities – that I quite literally need in my daily life were birthed from evil. As I drove to the store and reflected on this conversation, I was once again overwhelmed with gratitude for what God had done.

I left my gratitude in the car when we entered the bookstore, focusing instead on the task at hand: cashing in gift cards for some new books. In the accomplishment of this task, one of my daughter's persistent defiance resulted in a consequence for her: forfeiting the opportunity to get a new book for herself. This created an opportunity for my other daughter; with extra funds available, she could either choose an additional book for herself or purchase a book to bless someone else. She chose the latter, asking the cashier if she could return momentarily after choosing a book to bless someone. Touched by her choice, the cashier purchased the book she had wanted for herself and handed it to her. She was beaming as she clutched this gift, and my other daughter was very much not.

On the way home, my sweet rebel child said, "Mama, I am sorry for disobeying, but I'm glad I did. The only reason the man who works at the store was able to bless Sister was because I disobeyed. If I hadn't disobeyed, we would've bought my book and then we wouldn't have been able to bless someone else, and that man wouldn't have blessed Sister." She was right. Her disobedience cost her, but her sin presented an opportunity for her sister. In choosing honorably, blessings arose all around. The gratitude I left in the car when we parked at the bookstore returned as I marveled at how quickly my seven-year-old was able to see the beauty made from ashes.

God's backward way of doing things is woven into the small things, like a trip to the bookstore, and the big things, like traumatic events. While I may wonder why the bad sometimes has to happen in order for good to follow, I am confident – as I have learned through enduring trials of many kinds – that the good is much sweeter when it is birthed from that which was intended to harm.

Backward is His way, and it is oh-so beautiful.

DAILY REFLECTION

When we look at Joseph's story, we see years of him living in the gray area between evil and its turnaround to glory. His words in Genesis 50:20 were spoken from a place of hindsight, as he was looking God's Romans 8:28 nature in the face and seeing how each day of his oppression and imprisonment was used for the orchestration of good. Though we don't read of it in Scripture, I think it is safe to say that even Joseph struggled in his years of living in the gray area. Yet, each of those years had great purpose in his story, in the history of Egypt, and in the lineage of Jesus. They were necessary. Think of a specific event that serves as a pillar to your story. In what way can you speak the words of Genesis 50:20 about this event? If you are not on the other side of the gray yet, how can you use Joseph's story and faith as encouragement?

LET IT BURN

Beloved, do not be surprised at the fiery trial when it comes upon you to test you, as though something strange were happening to you. But rejoice insofar as you share Christ's sufferings, that you may also rejoice and be glad when His glory is revealed.
1 Peter 4:12-13 (ESV)

It is easy for me to rejoice in beauty. For one, it's beautiful, and beautiful things are naturally joyful. Beauty also contains more obvious evidence of God's handiwork, love, and care. The ashes are when praise can be hard to come by. The fire that precedes them, too.

I recall a documentary I watched a couple of years ago. I learned that all forests, regardless of their size, depend on fire in order to thrive. A number of conifers seal their cones with resin, which has to be burned away in order for the seeds to germinate. Out of the ashes of a forest fire, new life begins.

Forest fires are destructive and devastating. They

displace people, and their fumes bring residual damage. While the trees are burning, no one is thinking about the new life that will eventually burst through the soil as a result of the damage. On the contrary, all are thinking about the danger and damage while trying to cope with shock.

Refining fires are similar. They destroy, they bring a sense of displacement through discomfort, and there are residual effects in their wake. I cannot speak for others, but I certainly struggle to consider the new life that will come from the ashes of refinement while undergoing its flame. I instead find myself groaning, worrying about what is happening and what the future will look like, and trying to keep my anxiety in check.

It isn't until I see new life bursting forth that I am reminded of the beauty of the burning. At that moment, I am finally ready to look backward; to reflect on each stage of the prolonged growth of the forest, on its diversified purpose, and on the reason for its burning.

DAILY REFLECTION

When you consider your growth, what did the refining fire have to burn in order for that growth to take place? When you consider the trials you have endured, what growth can you identify that resulted from it?

Now, let's go a bit deeper. Recall a specific time when you found your life in a state of burning. In the midst of it, were you able to see beyond the flames, the pain, the destruction? Did you have hope?

It isn't until I see new life bursting forth that I am reminded of the beauty of the burning. At that moment, I am finally ready to look backward, to reflect on each stage of the prolonged growth of the forest, on its diversified purpose, and on the reason for its burning.

DAY TWELVE
BEAUTY IN SURRENDER

Therefore, I urge you, brothers and sisters, in view of God's mercy, to offer your bodies as a living sacrifice, holy and pleasing to God - this is your true and proper worship.
Romans 12:1

I will never tire of the beauty that autumn brings. Annually, I am awestruck by the artistry that borders the streets and trails, colors the hills, and coats our neighborhoods in color. What fascinates me the most about this annual manifestation of Glory is that the most beautiful time in a tree's life (in my humble opinion) is the time before death and dormancy.

In my fascination, I wonder why it is that God designed our forests to showcase such rich variances in color before stripping them bare for months. I wonder why it is that He calls our attention to the woodlands just before they lay their beauty to rest and stand disrobed before us. And then, I realize: our eyes are drawn to beauty, and there is indescribable beauty in surrender.

The trees are surrendered. They have control neither over their life cycle, nor over the timing of the seasons, nor over the color their leaves showcase when their production of chlorophyll slows. They simply are, and God simply does. And while He does, we marvel. We marvel at their transformation, we marvel at the beauty in their death.

But when it is our turn to surrender, do we? Do we simply "be" so God can simply do? Do we marvel as He does? Do we marvel at our transformation, at the beauty in our death?

Or do we fight it? Do we prolong the process because we think there is a better option than surrender or because we refuse to be ready when He calls?

DAILY REFLECTION

After considering the questions on the previous page, respond to the questions that follow, digging deep.

Do you view yourself as a living sacrifice that belongs to Jesus, or do you make choices based on your unconscious or conscious desires? What evidence do you have of this? In what ways can you surrender yourself to His will for you? If it is helpful, use the questions on the previous page to guide your reflection.

There is indescribable
beauty in surrender.

DAY THIRTEEN
REMNANTS

My Son, give me your heart and let your eyes delight in my ways.
Proverbs 23:26

Each spring, after winter has thawed and the sounds of new life begin to fill the space, there are remnants of autumn. Albeit few, they are there: brown, withered, stubborn leaves that never made their way to the forest floor. Most trees do not adorn them, but my eyes always pause on those that do. In the past, I've wondered why a few dozen leaves remained while hundreds more rode the wind to a place of rest for the winter.

While I'm sure there is some scientific explanation for it, I am even more certain that, often, it's as if I strive to be like those trees. I fight Him, grasping whatever it is He is calling me to release, refusing to let Him make beauty from something I just can't seem to part with. Maybe it is because I don't trust that He will make it beautiful in the way I wish He would. Maybe it is because I am simply not ready to be finished with it, so I hold fast to it. Or even still, maybe it is because I am selfish, I want my way, and that includes retaining my pride and not fully surrendering to Him.

Regardless of the justification I could tack onto it, if I choose to fight God in this way, when the new season comes with its beauty ready to bloom, I will have dead, dried remnants of the past that stand in the way of the new growth He has in store for me. If I withhold something from Him in my heart, I withhold the opportunity for Him to make beauty bloom.

DAILY REFLECTION

Releasing things can produce feelings of fear, anxiety, and insecurity. Whatever we have actually belongs to God, yet knowing this doesn't necessarily make releasing it to Him easy. What are you holding onto that He is asking you to release to Him? Is it a person, a situation, a dream, unresolved pain from your past, justice that hasn't been seen here on earth? Why do you think you're holding onto it? What is prohibiting you from letting your eyes delight in His ways? Whatever it is, He will wait patiently for you...but on the other side of that release is a gift that is far better than you can imagine.

If I choose to fight God when the new season comes with its beauty ready to bloom, I will have dead, dried remnants of the past that stand in the way of the new growth He has in store for me.

DAY FOURTEEN
ANOTHER LAP

Let Him.
Song of Songs 1:2a

An unexpected opportunity to be alone presented itself recently, which included an unexpected return to the "normal route" on my trail. Despite having taken that same path in the same direction for ninety-eight percent of my hikes there during the last two years, this time I hardly recognized it. The fallen leaves can do that to a place, but I sensed this was deeper than just aesthetics.

It was.

Brought once again to a place of swirling thoughts, I was fascinated that I seemed lost, in a sense, while wondering why God wanted me to go forward this time instead of backward, and while welcoming to mind something I once learned about shepherds and their sheep.

The mountains where shepherds lead their sheep are steep. Naturally, the safe way to climb involves walking around and around the mountain at a gradually higher elevation each lap. Having climbed plenty of mountains in my lifetime, I know that their surroundings changed very little with each lap around the mountain. While they were not on the same exact path they were on the last lap, it was quite similar to where they once walked.

Such is my situation. While I am not walking precisely the same path I have before, it is similar - just a little higher up, a little closer to the mountaintop. Sometimes things look and sound familiar, sometimes things feel familiar, and sometimes that sense of familiarity brings me back to a place I don't necessarily wish to return to.

I was brought back to two such places while my thoughts swirled; two places that changed the trajectory of my life, left many scars and wounds, and that still impact my daily life more than I wish they would. Then I was brought back to a third place, a place I do wish to return to. A place I hope to return to one day soon. A place where those scars, open wounds, and the impact of the blast still exist but are cared for tenderly. It is in that third place that I finally see the mountaintop, where the familiarity is behind me, and the redeeming love of the Shepherd I've been following around

and around the mountain rests on me once and for all...
because it is in that third place that I finally let Him.

DAILY REFLECTION

When you reflect on your life, past or present, are there similar situations, relationships, or struggles? Has it ever seemed like you're on the thousandth lap around the same mountain? Why do you think He has had you walk the same thing over and over again? What commonalities do the situations have? What growth have you experienced? Where have those paths led you? How has He cared for you during the journey?

DAY FIFTEEN

JOY SHIFT

Let us run with perseverance the race marked out for us, fixing our eyes on Jesus, the Pioneer and Perfecter of faith. For the joy set before Him He endured the cross, scorning its shame, and sat down at the right hand of the throne of God. Consider Him who endured such opposition from sinners, so that you will not grow weary and lose heart.
Hebrews 12:1b-3

Our minds are slippery places. Once a thought enters, it isn't long before a hundred of its companions join it and lead us down a path we can't retrace. The path of things I could say, think, and focus on for each of the places of pain I was brought back to yesterday is endless.

Historically, that is what I have chosen to do. Despite knowing the truth behind the five words in the opening quote, and despite knowing how slippery the admittance of just one measly thought is, I have chosen to let it in. While I cannot retrace the steps of the countless trains of thought I've allowed my mind to embark on, I can retrace the steps to the core of all of the thoughts: pain.

Today I played basketball with my youngest daughter. Sharper than should be allowed at her age, she faked an injury because she has observed that doing so results in a pause in the game and a restart with the ball. An advantageous (and manipulative) move, once she saw that this resulted favorably for her, she tried it again and again. The focus of our time on the court shifted from joy to pain, the latter eventually outweighing the former.

So it has been with the pain in my heart. Focusing on it has brought a sense of satisfaction. I have felt justified in allowing myself to experience this pain because I know that what happened was undeniably wrong. And so I - unconsciously or not - have chosen to hone in on the pain again and again. Before I realize it, the focus of my time has shifted from complete joy to complete pain, and soon after, the frequency and severity of that pain multiplies because I crave even more satisfaction.

It took walking her chosen path for my daughter to realize that, ultimately, her choice didn't result in the long-lasting joy she thought it would. What she actually experienced was fleeting. Likewise, it has taken me walking the path I have chosen for myself to realize that, ultimately, my choices haven't resulted in the long-lasting joy I thought they would. I too, must come to terms with my decisions -

even the seemingly innocent ones like which thoughts I ponder - and shift my focus.

DAILY REFLECTION

Keep a notepad and pen or your phone handy today, and write down your thoughts throughout the day - good, bad, and everything in between. Later on, sit down and review them. What did you allow your mind to focus on today? Did your thoughts honor God? We could all use refinement in this area; ask God to reveal a plan of action for you to take your thoughts captive and make them obedient to Him. Maybe it's a quick prayer, maybe it's a confession, maybe it's what I do with my daughters: give three praises about the very thing that was complained about.

DAY SIXTEEN
MISS INDEPENDENT

If you say, "The Lord is my refuge," and you make the most high your dwelling,
no harm will overtake you, no disaster will come near your tent.
For He will command His angels concerning you to guard you in all your ways;
they will lift you up in their hands, so that you will not strike your foot against a stone.
You will tread on the lion and the cobra; you will trample the great lion and the serpent.
Psalm 91:9-13

"Miss Independent." A phrase featured on memes, the title of a few songs from my youth, and words I'd use to describe myself, I would also render this coupling of words to be one of my greatest internal battles. Independence can be a defense mechanism, and for me, that rings true often.

Recently, a prayer warrior told me that the way I am now - independent, self-sufficient, and essentially always in beast mode - is a result of what I've survived. It made complete sense to me that day, but today brought revelation at a new depth as it wed so many things my Heavenly Father has been revealing to me.

It began with another date with my trail. Every time I hike, I check the signs on each post along the way as if I were a rookie. Yet, only today did I notice that the "backward way" God has been prompting me to take is actually the way that is numbered chronologically. That is, my "forward way" is actually the true wrong way. From my very first steps on that path to this day, I have walked as if the route I take is the only route. Thankfully, my clueless and, at times, ignorant self is loved by a patient and gracious God.

The revelation continued in the car. Through the voice of Kelly Clarkson, God reminded me of many things He has spoken, revealed, and convicted me of...self-sufficiency, apprehension, an open door, leaving old habits behind, changing misconceptions, going in a new direction. Each lyric unraveled the pride that once fueled my voice as I sang them years ago. This time, I sang from a place of revelation, a place where I am beginning to understand who I am at a new depth and how all of the things that have been a part of my story have not only served their purpose but have helped to bring me to the exact place I am now: still Miss Independent, but now I am independent of protecting myself, for that is the job of my Heavenly Father.

DAILY REFLECTION

Look back on the list of traits you made on day four. Focusing on the positive and on those that surface frequently, reflect on your life and try to connect those traits back to things you experienced. What experiences helped shape who you are today? Do you tend to use those traits in a God-honoring way, or does pride hinder Him from showing you how to glorify Him by employing those traits in His way? In your reflection, what areas jump out at you that need refinement, surrender, and grace?

Independence can be a defense
mechanism and for me that rings true
often.

DAY SEVENTEEN
ONLY EVER GOOD

Praise the Lord, my soul, all my inmost being,
praise His holy name,
Praise the Lord, my soul, and forget not all His benefits - who forgives
all your sins and heals all your diseases,
who redeems your life from the pit and crowns you with love and
compassion,
who satisfies your desires with good things so that your youth is
renewed like the eagle's.
Psalm 103:1-5

Two of my favorite words in Scripture are found in Song of Songs 1:2: "Let Him." Each time my eyes fall upon them, each time they come to mind, or each time they are spoken, I stand in the middle of a beautiful collision of simplicity and complication.

In the Bible courses I teach, I often speak of the denotation and connotation of words. One serves as the more "official" of meanings, whereas the other can be the cultural or personal definition of a word. I explain to my students that the connotations of words typically branch off and connect to our emotions and experiences with those words. The collision that surrounds me consists of those two things: the simplicity of what two simple words truly mean, and the complication I experience when I bask in their meaning to me. Quite literally, "let Him" means to not prevent the Creator and Ruler of the universe.

Historically, my experience with these words has consisted of an initial acceptance of them, and then a recounting of all of the strife, pain, suffering, betrayal, and trauma I have walked through in life. I have wavered between knowing with my entire being that my God does not cause that evil but births beauty from its ashes and stepping a little too far into those dark moments. When I have stepped too far into them, I have doubted - or forgotten - His goodness. But I know that I know that I KNOW - He is only ever good.

He allows sin to occur knowing the consequences of it and knowing the choices we will make as a result of it. He knows who will choose to continue in that sin and who will subsequently have to walk away because of that person's choice to remain in sin. He knows where He will lead us from there, who He will lead us to, and He knows all of the wonders of our futures because He has prepared them.

If I am not careful to recognize His goodness with praise and thanksgiving, and if I am not careful to find the joy in the way He uses the fallenness of this world for His glorious purposes, I will step back into the depravity of my story and forget His goodness. I must let Him do what He does - which is only ever good - and praise Him as He does it.

DAILY REFLECTION

Write down the first thing that comes to mind after reading this question: What is the most painful experience you have endured to date? After recording the details of this experience and how it impacted you, consider this question: How have you "let Him" (in other words, how have you not prevented the Creator and Ruler of the universe) in it? Highlight His goodness in that experience; no matter how difficult it is or how long it takes you, seek that goodness until you find it. If you're not there yet, don't fret - come back when you do. And then, praise Him!

If I am not careful to recognize
His goodness with praise and
thanksgiving. and if I am not careful
to find the joy in the way He uses the
fallenness of this world for His
glorious purposes. I will step back
into the depravity of my story and
forget His goodness.

DAY EIGHTEEN
RESTRUCTURING REQUIRED

Por fe también, aunque Sara no podía tener hijos y Abraham no era demasiado viejo, éste recibió fuerzas para ser padre, porque creyó que Dios cumpliría sin falta su promesa.
Hebreos 11:11 (DHH94PC)

And by faith, even Sarah, who was past childbearing age, was enabled to bear children because she considered Him faithful who had made the promise.
Hebrews 11:11

I am learning that the wonders God has prepared for us require a few things: our surrender ("letting Him"), His refining and equipping of us, and His orchestration of whatever it is He is walking us into. Today, He fixed my heart on what I receive when I - by faith - surrender and let Him.

Two words of a Spanish translation of Hebrews 11:11 read, "he received 'fuerzas'" in English. Receiving immediately makes me think of a gift, which I have to be open to and accepting of in order to receive it. In other words, this is the "let" part. A quest into the meaning of "fuerzas" led me to many definitions (capacity, vigor, or robustness needed to move something heavy or that is resistant; power or authority; etc.), but one piqued my interest more than the others: "an action or influence that can modify the movement or structure of a body." "Modify the structure of a body," which, in this case, is received.

I cannot enter into the fulfillment of His promise to me built as I am now any more than Abraham (or Sarah, for that matter) could have entered into the fulfillment of His promise to them built as they were. Like what needed to be done with them, I need to be restructured. And while the application of this interpretation is quite literal for them, it is not so literal for me.

His restructuring of me is relative to my wiring. A system that is quite literally out of my control leads me to a place of wanting to be in control, and being in control is not only unhealthy but unholy. If I am in control, I am not letting Him, but am instead an obstacle to myself and to receiving the fulfillment of His promise to me.

The simple answer to the question, "How do I receive this restructuring?" is: surrender. But I can't stop at simplicity; I must consider what surrender looks like for me. I must embrace the simplicity of it while considering the intricacies. My entrance to this season of receiving beckons my preparedness, and my preparedness requires restructuring.

DAILY REFLECTION

In the process of Abraham and Sarah's waiting for the fulfillment of a prayer-turned-promise, Sarah grew impatient and took control. While God remained faithful to His promise to them, there were repercussions to her choice. What promise(s) has God made to you that you are waiting for Him to fulfill? Do you trust that He will provide all that is needed – including whatever restructuring is required in you – for it? Where are you taking control that you shouldn't be?

If I am in control, I am not letting Him but am instead an obstacle to myself and to receiving the fulfillment of His promise to me.

DAY NINETEEN
TAKE A BOW

Very truly I tell you, unless a kernel of wheat falls to the ground and dies, it remains only a single seed. But if it dies, it produces many seeds.
John 12:24

A couple of weeks ago, we retired our garden for the year. In the middle of ripping it out, I took special notice of our basil plant. There were sprigs that had gone to flower, and, at that time, had dried up. I pinched a sprig to remove it - not paying attention to the fact that my fingers were squeezing a dried flower - and felt something firm between my fingers. When I opened them, there were tiny black seeds stuck to my skin. Intrigued, I snapped off the sprig and began to study it.

An herb plant grows and grows until it reaches the point of, as I call it, "going to flower." It is at that point that that particular branch, or sprig, is finished producing the herb. And it is at that point that the seeds are produced.

The production of seeds has always fascinated me. After a branch has produced all that it is intended to, a beautiful flower emerges. It's like the capstone of the plant's purpose. Then, upon dying, the flower produces seeds that will start the miraculous story all over again. The basil sprig brought that fascination to a different level because of its uniqueness. It also provided me with the answer to the question I was pondering here yesterday before I even knew I would need it.

I brought several of the dried sprigs to school with me the next day. As a part of our lesson for the day, I asked my students to make observations about them. I also asked them to show me in which direction they thought the sprig had been growing. Every one of them got it wrong.

After the flower blooms, it droops forward as it dies, as if it were bowing. In doing so, its seeds – which are incredibly tiny – take advantage of gravity to fall into the soil so they can produce new life. My students were justifiably mistaken about the plant's direction of growth because the degree to which these flowers bowed was so great that it looked like they were perched up toward the sun.

This is what I am called to do when I surrender. Not only do I have to die to myself, but I must do so with reverence; I, like the plant from my garden, shall bow before my Father. It is only then that the seeds He has cultivated in me are able to fall into the soil so they can produce the life that will grow in the next season.

In life as a whole and in the small things, this is what I am called to do. This is the way I receive my restructuring.

DAILY REFLECTION

For so long I looked more like Jacob in the Old Testament than I did my basil plant, thrashing about because I was too stubborn and prideful to let go of what I thought was best. It is one thing to surrender once you have lost a wrestling match, like Jacob did, but it is quite different to surrender and bow in reverence before the person you are surrendering to. Reflect on a time - past or present - when you dug your heels in on something. Did you turn out like Jacob, with a battle scar, or did God let you off scot-free? Explore what was fueling your pride and stubbornness. Have you handed that to our Jesus, or is it still a struggle? What did you glean from this experience that you can take with you and actively apply in the present day and future? How can you encourage others using your battle wound (or lack thereof)?

DAY TWENTY
HIS ORDER

But the moment one turns to the Lord with an open heart, the veil is lifted and they see.
2 Corinthians 3:16 (TPT)

God has a specific order that things happen in: His order. If the flower bowed after it dried, it would crumble apart. If the flower and seeds came before the fruit, what would the point of the plant be?

I spend a lot of time trying to make sense of His order, but typically only when it comes to me and my life. I'll excitedly admire His order in Creation and in other people's lives, but when it comes to what He wants to do in me, I turn into a full-blown investigator and try to figure out His method before He wants me to see it.

A song delivered this beautiful conviction to my heart this morning. As it told of God's wonderful generosity, it had the recipe for receiving spelled out in a different way - a deeper way. And, as I'm sure you could guess, I have been approaching it backward.

My investigation is accomplished through action. I look for things, listen for things, and contemplate things. When I do so, my eyes search frantically instead of looking where they should be. My hands are typically clenched in distress or frustration, most often because I just can't seem to figure it out. Certainly, my heart is not open at any point in this "necessary" action; how could it be when I have already decided I know what is needed?

The truth of the matter is that I can't receive when my heart is closed off, when my hands are not open, and when I am looking elsewhere. The lyrics have it right - I cannot see the goodness of God with my own eyes if I do not receive it. I cannot receive what He has for me if my hands are not open. I cannot open my hands if I do not open my heart first. Heart, hands, eyes. That is His order.

And to that, I die to myself, I bow in reverence, and I wait...heart, hands, and eyes as He wishes.

DAILY REFLECTION

Spiritually speaking, what is the status of your heart, your hands, and your eyes? Which of the three do you struggle with most: a heart that is open to whatever His plan/gift is, hands that are not clinging to other things, or open eyes to see His goodness? Invite the Holy Spirit to search your heart and lead you to whatever it is that is causing you to struggle there. Once you've arrived, process it out here with Him.

DAY TWENTY-ONE

PARADE REST

Be still before the Lord and wait patiently for Him.
Psalm 37:7a

I spent my high school years on our school's dance team. Every year we went to a UDA camp in the summer to learn new dances, have fun and bond, and to compete. We always played a game called "Drill Downs" that required incredible discipline and focus. A Simon Says-type game, military commands such as "atten-hut," "hand salute," and "parade rest," were called out and you had to follow them promptly, completely, and precisely. The last dancer standing won.

I was good at Drill Downs. It was easy for me to tune everything out and hone in on the voice calling out the drills. It was easy for me to maintain control over my body, mind, and emotions so that I was ready to do exactly what that voice said at exactly the right time. It was easy for me to execute things precisely because I was a perfectionist.

For me, the greatest challenge came with the command "parade rest." With your hands behind your back, your head down, and your eyes fixated on the floor, you are unable to move from parade rest until the command "atten-hut" is called; any other movement means you are out of the game. This presented the greatest challenge for me because the waiting, the stillness, and the silence brought anxiety. I battled with wondering what would be called next, when it would be called, and how many other people were left standing. Anxiety came in the resting, the stillness, and the waiting. But once another drill was called - even if it were four or five called back-to-back, I was golden; it was easy for me to obey in rapid succession once I started moving.

Twenty years later, there is still a voice that calls out drills, it is just not that of a UDA dancer. It is the voice of my Abba Father. And, twenty years later, I am not as good at Drill Downs. I struggle to tune everything out and hone in on God's voice, primarily because, most of the time, my own is much louder. It is difficult for me to maintain control over my body, mind, and emotions, which means I can't do what He says at exactly the right time. And despite still being a perfectionist (though now I would more accurately label myself as a "perfectionist who relaxes at times") - I don't always have confidence in my ability to execute His calling of me precisely.

Today, He called out a drill. It was the first time in quite a while that I was able to tune everything out and hone in on His voice. Because I was a bit emotional and my mind was running rampant, I sought wisdom regarding acting on His drill and received double confirmation. And as obeyed, He called out something else to do in conjunction with it.

In the moments before He called out this first drill, I felt as I did twenty years ago while in parade rest in the gym at Western Michigan University. I sensed He would speak, but I wasn't sure what He would say or when He would say it. Once He did, it was easy to obey - even with drills coming in succession - because I had already begun to move. And after precisely executing the two drills He called out, He called me to return to the place I still dislike the most: parade rest.

Waiting in parade rest feels similar to what it felt like twenty years ago, but I know He will speak again. The fact that I don't know what or when He will still isn't comforting, but I know that if I remain at rest, with my heart and my hands open to receive, He will call out another drill.

DAILY REFLECTION

Do you struggle in the times of quiet stillness, or in the times of great action? What causes you to struggle? What is God trying to show or say to you during those times, through and in spite of any anxiety or negative emotion you may experience?

DAY TWENTY-TWO
REMAIN IN REPETITION

For God does speak - now one way, now another - though no one
perceives it.
Job 33:14

Sometimes during Drill Downs, the same drill is repeated three, four, or more times. Following that repetition, a different drill is called out. The purpose of the heavy repetition before a new drill is to try to trick the participants so they mess up and are thus out of the game.

God does the same thing, sometimes, but His heart isn't to trick us so we mess up and are "out." In my experience, He often has us do the same thing over and over again before calling us to do something that is brand new to us. Perhaps His purpose in this is that something within that practice is needed for the new thing, so we need to hone that skill through repetition. Perhaps His purpose is that we struggle to do what He says when He says to, so we need to practice unconditional and immediate obedience. Even still, His purpose may be that He wants to shock and surprise us as we leave that place of repetition with something new.

Unlike Drill Downs, God repeats His drills using various avenues, all driven by the Holy Spirit. My repetitive drill to rest has recently been called out more loudly than ever - through the way my life is (nonstop, unpredictable, more than I can manage on my own as a working single mom of two), through my devotional the last two mornings, and now through an occurrence that could only have been orchestrated by my Abba Father.

One of His repeats came this morning, by way of my mentor. She attended my church's Prayer House to receive prayer for herself and her family. When the person leading prayer began, she mentioned the name "Amanda" and asked if there was any connection for anyone. After my mentor raised her hand, a man was asked to speak a word over me. The word was plentiful, but the main point was the repetitive drill God has called out to me: "Stop overthinking and jumping to conclusions. Let go, rest, and allow me to do what only I can do."

While I am not necessarily joyful that I need to have

this repeated to me, I will take as many repetitions as He gives. Each and every one is a gift-wrapped assurance - assurance that He sees me, He hears me, and He loves me - so much so that He goes to the lengths He did today, placing people strategically so that even when I am not physically there, He can speak to my heart.

And until He reveals whatever it is that He is doing, I will remain in the repetition of rest and surrender.

DAILY REFLECTION

I think we often define divine miracles as major events like healing or drastic life changes. Everything God does is miraculous, including the varying ways He speaks to us. How has God spoken to you? How has He shown Himself to you?

DAY TWENTY-THREE
EXPECTANT

I lift up my eyes to the mountains - where does my help come from?
My help comes from the Lord, the maker of Heaven and earth.
Psalm 121:1-2

My perfectionism benefitted me at dance camp, but now it can be one of my most hindering traits. Upon finishing writing one of these entries, I hit "enter" twice, change the text to bold, and write the next number. I've not thought twice about this, perhaps because it is insignificant at surface level. Today, it caused me to pause.

This began as a forty-day journey. I had a clear message from God to commune with Him because He had work to do in my heart. I knew that this - seeking Him and processing my healing with Him through words - was His chosen avenue for the transformation of my heart. I counted the days on my calendar and I set out with an end in sight (September 10th was the 40th day).

A lover of structure and order, I was adamant that there could only be one thing per day that I recorded here. It made complete sense to me: God would give me one revelation per day for forty days and I would write about it. Organized with a timeline and a structure, I set out (I wonder what my heart, hands, and eyes looked like back then).

Faithful to this self-imposed structure initially, my flesh and inability to do things one hundred percent His way grew to be an obstacle, which led me away from what He called me to and into a well of distraction. The distractions I entertained prevented me from engaging in this, but in His goodness, He used them. Through them, He broke down walls that prevented His Truth from penetrating the lies I was harboring in my heart. Without walls, I returned to His calling of me, this time without the self-imposed structure with which I began. And when I returned, the next space for revelation was waiting for me because when I left, I left demonstrating my expectancy of His faithfulness: I had written the number for the next day.

Chewing on all of this, I can hear His whisper: "Amanda, you wrote and still write the next number. You know I will provide. You know my heart. You know how I love you. Your faith - your typing of those numbers - evidences that. I have accounted for all things, even those that are not part of my intended will. I love you too much to allow those things to change any of the plans I have for you. Continue with me. Seek me and I will show you. Rest in my presence."

He is right. I did write the next number in anticipation of more goodness. What was birthed from a trait I have as a result of my trauma was used as a reminder that I know where my help comes from: My Abba.

DAILY REFLECTION

Recall a time when you persisted in doing things your own way. Why do you think it is that we are so stubborn about maintaining control? When we persist in doing things our own way, do we actually have and demonstrate faith in Him? How do we choose faith over the driver's seat? How do we allow God to help us? Reflect on and respond to these questions in light of the instance you recalled from your own life.

DAY TWENTY-FOUR
MY BACKWARD IS HIS FORWARD

I am the vine; you are the branches. Whoever abides in me and I in Him, He it is that bears much fruit, for apart from me you can do nothing.
John 15:5 (ESV)

I love being alone. I love quiet. I love allowing my mind to wander, to ponder things I otherwise may not if I were in the company of others. I am called to fellowship. I am called to walk with others and to mutually build, sharpen, and love. Yet, solitude would be my first choice. Historically, it has been. There have certainly been seasons where I have been called to solitude and others where I have chosen it because I knew it was the only way for me to get to the other side of something. Despite my profound love of people and the fulfillment I have in connecting deeply with them, I love being alone.

Because of that desire, it is uncanny that I have been

battling with finishing this fellowship with God in a setting of solitude. Initially, I welcomed the isolation. Lately, though, I have felt free from that. I have felt pulled toward others, toward immersion in specific, deep fellowship. Ironically, since I felt that pull, He has been revealing through other people what He wants me to know. Fellowship is His method of choice for revelation, which is completely backward to me. Thankfully, at this point I am well-versed that my backward is His forward.

I cannot readily accept the prophetic Word given to my mentor for me (from a service I wasn't even present for!) without having fellowship with my mentor. I cannot have a repetition of another prophetic Word given to me directly from a dear friend without having fellowship with her. I cannot have confirmation of another repetitive Word given to me by a mentee without having fellowship with her. Yet I cannot find meaning in any of this if I do not invest in time alone with my Abba Father.

Fellowship is necessary for our walk because God is a God of relationship. Solitude is necessary for our walk because God is a God of relationship. God is necessary for our walk because He is a God of relationship. Ultimately, it all comes back to Him. In the quiet and in the noise, in the distraction-free and the chaos, it all comes back to Him.

DAILY REFLECTION

Do you prefer to be alone or with others? What is challenging for you in each of those settings? How has God moved in each for you?

Fellowship is necessary for our walk
because God is a God of relationship

Solitude is necessary for our walk
because God is a God of relationship

God is necessary for our walk
because He is a God of relationship

DAY TWENTY-FIVE
FLOOD AND DROUGHT

Drought comes when God withholds rain; floods come when He turns water loose.
Job 12:15 (GNT)

For several years, I lived in Tucson, where there is persistent drought outside of monsoon season. In monsoon season, the rain comes in fast and falls hard, the floods rush in, and then slowly dissipate, while the remaining hours of the day are extreme - in both heat and dryness.

One Saturday afternoon during monsoon season, I went hiking with a friend from work. He was extremely familiar with the Catalina Mountains and hiking in the desert, so naturally, it was easy to trust him. We both knew a monsoon was inevitable because of the season, but we anticipated it wouldn't hit until after our descent.

This particular trail was not what I was accustomed

to; instead of dirt and sand, it consisted of flat, smooth rocks – at least in the area we were in when the rains hit. We had already begun our descent, but we were too late. We faced a decision with two dangerous options: descend in the storm atop slippery rocks or remain on the mountain where lightning could, and likely would, strike. We decided to stay and sought shelter in a nook created by some fallen rock until the monsoon passed and it was safe to descend.

On a different Saturday – this time in the morning – we tackled another peak. It was June, which, in Arizona, means the dry heat is extreme. I always brought water with me, but this day I didn't bring enough in my pack. The challenge that particular peak presented combined with my lack of water resulted in an inability to perform as I normally would, both physically and mentally. I was dizzy, disoriented, and weak. The only thing that got me through that hike was knowing we had more water in the car.

Much like we experience the drought and flooding of the desert and their respective effects, we can experience the drought and flooding of Truth. We writers refer to the drought as "writer's block." It is our arch nemesis and is certainly something I have experienced. In the past, it has frustrated me greatly, mostly because I put undue pressure on myself to meet deadlines, follow a certain structure, or perform a certain way.

I realized today that I have not experienced writer's block since committing to this project. In fact, today I was in a monsoon of revelation; within a seventy-five-minute timespan, five vastly different messages were delivered to my heart. In contrast, I have vivid memories of late nights in front of my iMac, pleading with myself to produce something in the midst of a photojournalism project. It is hard to believe the woman in front of the keyboard at that time is the same one that could hardly stop writing today.

Certainly, I am not immune to writer's block just because I am a few years older than the last time it plagued me. In fact, I would venture to say that the weeks I spent avoiding this project could count as writer's block. What I have come to realize is that writers don't knowingly prevent the flow of truth; none of us desire to be incapable of expressing the deep longings of our hearts. Yet because we are human it will inevitably happen, and because it is inevitable we have to learn to work with it as it comes.

As such, I embrace the flood of Truth when it pours as I embraced the monsoon rains that day, and I wait expectantly through the drought as I anticipated its end - and the water that awaited me - once before.

DAILY REFLECTION

Have you persevered equally through the times of flood and drought? Is one season easier than the other for you? Why do you think that is?

DAY TWENTY-SIX

A DANDELION'S SURRENDER

Therefore go out from their midst, and be separate from them, says the Lord.
2 Corinthians 6:17a (ESV)

There was a dandelion - its stem balancing on the edge of a glass - on my kitchen counter when I got home last night. A normal sight in my kitchen during the spring and summer, I was perplexed to find it there at the beginning of November. I was not perplexed that it was closed up and beginning to shrivel, though. It was out of its element, and what can thrive that way?

That same dandelion caught my attention while preparing dinner today, due to its appearance. It was open, robust and bright, and appeared to be thriving. It also was no longer hanging over the edge of the glass; its stem was fully immersed in the water. In between mouthfuls of pasta, my daughter excitedly shared every detail of this dainty flower's story during dinner. From its discovery to its transformation, from closed to in bloom, and from its current position in a glass to planning its future (apparently we are starting a dandelion farm), she was a reel of unstoppable joy.

All the while, the only thing I could think about was how this meek plant had surrendered.

Winter is approaching, there are no insects flying about to benefit from its arrival, and the only flowers in bloom (at least around these parts) are potted mums. It is not time for dandelions to burst through the soil. This dainty yellow flower was a lone ranger in the withering grass and carpet of fallen leaves.

While absorbing her joy, I pondered how its surrender ultimately would result in growth. I wondered how many times I have obstinately fought against growth because I didn't feel ready, because it intimidated me, or because I simply didn't want to do my part in it. I can't imagine bursting out of hiding and into an atmosphere that is unlike that which is ideal for my flourishing, at a time that is not agreeable to my existence, and doing so entirely alone - to the point where my standing out is inevitable. Yet that is exactly what happened with this flower.

As she planned our future with its seeds, I pondered

the generational blessing that comes from such surrender. I wondered how many times my surrender has been the avenue through which God has planted seeds in the hearts of my daughters, my nieces and nephews, my friends' children, or even my students. I basked in the beauty of that unknown, grateful for God's omniscient and omnipresent nature, always so meticulous in His planning and execution.

I returned to her planning of our gardening future with one conclusion: I want to be just like that dandelion, not just today, but always.

DAILY REFLECTION

I spent far too many years trying to blend in with the rest of the world. I wanted to look, talk, dress, and act like others instead of embracing my individuality and standing tall as myself. It was as foreign as that yellow flower trying to be a blade of grass, and I was absolutely miserable. In what ways have you denied yourself a life of being set apart? Why? What can you do going forward to stand tall in your identity? Revisit days three, four, and even sixteen to help you.

DAY TWENTY-SEVEN
LOVE'S IDENTITY

And He said: "Truly I tell you, unless you change and become like little children, you will never enter the Kingdom of Heaven."
Matthew 18:3

The persistent and quiet revelation woven into my days is that of love's identity. Something we almost eagerly overcomplicate with our desires, expectations, and insecurities (all while viewing it through the lens of our life experience), love's identity is truly as simple as the relationship between my daughter and that lone dandelion.

She saw beauty peeking through the ordinary. It beckoned to her simply by existing exactly as it was designed to. She reached out because she is love. She is so very much love that she can't contain it all within herself; she must share it. She is compelled to. She chose that flower and cared for it tenderly, perhaps not exactly the way it was designed to be cared for, but the way she knew how to. And she did so with love.

She adored that dandelion. The way she spoke of it exuded adoration – from how beautiful it was to how it blossomed to the hope she had for its future. Even her eyes demonstrated that adoration; it was impossible to not see her heart.

Her beloved dandelion has remained closed all day today, but her love remains open. Acknowledging its state, she anticipates what is to come and not just because she knows what follows this stage in a dandelion's life, but because love always hopes. And the love that has continuously and tenderly cared for this dandelion is because of one simple thing: choice. My daughter chose to see that flower. She chose to see its beauty instead of focusing on all the reasons it shouldn't be there. She chose to care for it instead of reasoning herself out of it, and she chose to care for it tenderly. She chooses to hope for what is coming instead of worrying about what may or may not come.

She chooses because she loves. She loves because she chooses. Reciprocal, interdependent, and simple. Love's identity is choice.

DAILY REFLECTION

Scripture is clear that child-like faith is what we are called to. So frequently, I have seen God's reasoning for this by simply watching children - both my own daughters and children of people I know. If you can recall instances where a child's faith and heart was demonstrated, record it here and write about what you can mirror from that in the days to come. If you cannot, I encourage you to pay attention in the coming days. I am confident you will see exactly what it is I am talking about, and when you do, I encourage you to come and write about what you can mirror from it.

She chooses because she loves.
She loves because she chooses.
Reciprocal, interdependent, and
simple. Love's identity is choice.

DAY TWENTY-EIGHT
EVICTING FEAR

There is no fear in love, but perfect love drives out fear, because fear has to do with punishment.
1 John 4:8a

One of love's greatest enemies is fear. Fear prohibits us from choosing because it paralyzes us. It forecasts every possibility for the future all at once, overwhelming us with anxiety. As if that weren't enough, it changes forms, methods, and appearance, making it difficult to identify.

Fear is something I've dealt with heavily in recent years. It has been a journey of discovery, facing hard truths, trekking through discomfort, and choosing differently – choosing love. Despite my efforts to understand and conquer fear, I often question myself (self-doubt is one of fear's favorite disguises), worrying that I have been blind or misunderstood something. Recently, I have been showered with revelation, and while my faith grows exponentially, self-doubt continues to take up residence in my mind.

Graced with fellowship with a dear friend this evening, we embarked on a healing prayer of sorts. As we began, I silently asked God to speak to me through my children, who were playing in a neighboring room with my friend's daughter. Within seconds, my youngest daughter shouted, "School's over!" She marched into our family room on her way upstairs, giggling profusely. Holding a children's dictionary of ours, she called my name, saying she had something to show me. I opened my eyes to see the page she had opened for me - a page that contained a drawing of a centipede. She erupted in laughter, telling me over and over again that it was a centipede. I sent her on her way and praised God for the two messages He delivered through her.

The end of a school day signifies that the learning for that day is finished. Students take what they have learned beyond the doors of the school building and apply it to whatever they face. My daughter's proclamation of the end of the school day signified that my time of learning has finished and it is time to apply what I have learned.

Her prop is what brought the second message. While dictionaries contain the official meanings of words, we also relate to words in a more personal manner, attaching our own meaning to them. Centipedes are one of the very few things in life that I fear. If I were to select an image to serve as the visual representation of fear for me, I'd most certainly choose a drawing just like the one she proudly displayed.

What was fun and games to her ministered to me. There is no reason for me to walk onward in self-doubt; not only do I have experiential knowledge of what fear is for me personally, I, too, have a Book that offers a clear understanding of what it is. The time has come for the application of my learning, for the removal of fear to create space for more love.

DAILY REFLECTION

My fear of centipedes began in childhood, and continues for the same reasons today. Centipedes bring me fear for many reasons. They're hideous (sorry, God), they're insanely fast, they always catch you by surprise, and if you don't kill them, they go into hiding underneath who knows what until they're ready to catch you by surprise again. No thanks.

What image would represent fear in your dictionary? What about that particular thing scares you? In what ways does (or could) what you fear minister to you?

Fear prohibits us from choosing because it paralyzes us.

DAY TWENTY-NINE
CLAP BACK

The thief comes only to steal and kill and destroy. I came that they may have life and have it abundantly.
John 10:10 (ESV)

Several months ago, I had a dream. In this dream, I had moved into an apartment, and shortly after moving my things in, I had to go somewhere. When I returned, I found that someone had broken in and stolen my camera and laptop. I panicked because these items were not only costly but they were the two items I needed to do what I am most passionate about: my camera for photography, and my laptop for writing and teaching. I investigated and learned who this repetitive thief in the apartment complex was. Once night fell, I set out, marched over to his apartment, snuck in, and took my stuff back.

I was perplexed for quite some time about what this

dream meant. I had had prophetic dreams that had come to fruition in real life before, but this one was different because it was about me. What did those two stolen items mean for me personally? I wondered if it meant that my passion would be taken, that I would lose my job, or that I would lose my talent and have to start over completely. In the last several weeks, I feel as if it has been pieced together for me.

At the very beginning of my walk with Jesus, I ventured on a 365 project. I took a photo every day for a year and shared it, along with whatever God had laid on my heart relative to what I had photographed. The project led me to the greatest growth and the deepest level of intimacy with Jesus I have ever experienced. I spent every day anticipating – expecting – Him to show Himself to me so I could document it, write about it, and share His heart with the world. This project required my camera and my computer – two items that are crucial for living out my God-given passion.

What I have come to see is that this dream wasn't about the photos, the writing, or the project; it was about the relational benefit that project yielded for me and Jesus. By stealing my camera, he was stealing the unique perspective God gave me, and by stealing my computer, the enemy was hindering my ability to use the gifts of language and teaching He gave me in order to share this perspective with others.

Without that perspective, without that ability for Him to use my words to reveal things to me for my growth, how could I get closer to Him?

As clearly as I can see the definition of "centipede" in the children's dictionary resting on our bookshelf, I now see the attempts of the enemy to steal what never belonged to him anyhow. And this – this daily fellowship with the Lord where I am writing so He can use my words for His glory – this is my clap back.

DAILY REFLECTION

I love John 10:10. Jesus reveals Satan's game plan and follows up with reassurance that He is here to do quite literally the exact opposite. It's a presentation of facts that leaves us in the same position I was in in my dream: a position of choice. What has the enemy stolen from you? What has he tried to kill or destroy? Have you - or are you - choosing a clap back? What would it look like for you to take back what was never his?

BLIND

*Such a person does not know the way to go, having been blinded by
the darkness.*
1 John 2:11b (NLT)

I have lived every day with an empty space in my
heart. Acutely aware of it yet oblivious to its cause, I have also
lived every day eager for it to be filled. I have pleaded with
God to restore the faith and trust I had in Him at the
beginning of my walk - the faith and trust that grew so
significantly during my 365 photo project. And as I further
consider the dream in which my camera and laptop were
stolen, I see more clearly that the empty space I have lived
with is directly connected to what had been stolen from me.

Since the gifts I use my camera and laptop for are
rooted in my perspective, losing those items had one primary
effect on me: blindness. And I lived for so long, absolutely

clueless that I couldn't see, because I didn't lose my physical eyesight, but rather became blind spiritually.

When I consider not being able to see, the challenges the physically blind face come to mind. It is overwhelming to consider the difficulties they face in everyday life. How do they have that much trust for drivers while crossing busy intersections? What do they do in facilities that only offer staircases? Are blind women unable to wear make-up because they can't see to apply it? How do they style their hair? In what ways are the blind limited in the workplace? How are they able to write?

I spend far less time considering the difficulties I face in everyday life by my spiritual blindness. I don't consider how the enemy distracts me from my path. I focus far too much on what is going on around me instead of what is going on within me. I panic instead of considering other routes when the one I face is not possible for me. I don't easily depend on others to help me do what I am unable to do. And, I either struggle to see my limitations, or they steal the show and distract me from what I should actually be focusing on.

I cannot imagine someone who is physically blind walking around in denial of their condition; there is great imminent danger in that. Yet how often do I walk around oblivious to my state of spiritual blindness? How often am I in utter denial of it? How often do I participate in the depletion of my vision, or put on blinders to shield myself from the Truth?

In order to complete the process, to regain lost ground, to restore my faith and trust in my Abba, to turn a clap back into applause, I must acknowledge the Truth about my condition: I was blind. Then and only then can I begin to restore my vision, regain my perspective, and – in turn – restore what has been lost.

DAILY REFLECTION

We all have blind spots or weaknesses. What are yours? Are they similar to what I have named for myself thus far: distractions, decision paralysis, hyper-independence, ignorance, or hyper-focus on limitations? Confess your blindness specifically – it is the first step toward restoration.

DAY THIRTY-ONE
SEEING ISN'T BELIEVING

Blessed are those who have not seen and yet have believed.
John 20:29b

Every morning on the way to school, we pray. Typically my oldest daughter prays first, my youngest follows her, and I close the prayer. Several weeks ago, my youngest daughter began starting her prayer with one sentence that has changed my approach to many things: "Heavenly, Father, I echo the prayer of Stasia and I echo the prayer that Mama is about to pray."

I have heard many people, myself included, echo the prayer of someone who has already prayed. However, she is the first person I have ever heard agree to a prayer that hasn't yet been prayed. How utterly beautiful it is that she trusts me and the Spirit in me so much that she agrees with my supplications before she ever hears them! It is a demonstration of blind faith – of trusting what is to come without having any idea what that might be – like I have never seen. And it is my example.

When I know someone's heart and the heart of my Father, I can trust. I can have blind faith, knowing that whatever they request in prayer will ultimately be in alignment with the will of my Abba because He is only ever good.

So what, then, is it that gets in the way of this for me that is not even a consideration for my daughter? The answer is: I have twenty-nine more years of allowing the enemy to throw shame at me, to alter my thinking, and to cultivate reactions that are the exact opposite of the ways of God than she does.

At the tender age of seven, my daughter certainly experiences attacks from the enemy, but she still has a strong grasp on her God-given identity. Whereas at the age of thirty-six, I work tirelessly to walk firmly in my God-given identity after all those years of allowing the enemy's arrows to pierce it. I work to undo what the enemy has worked on for over three decades, and ironically, that work consists of walking forth into each moment with blind faith.

DAILY REFLECTION

One of my greatest areas of struggle is the space between God's promise and seeing it come to fruition. Ultimately, that struggle is rooted in my not walking firmly in my identity, because I am entertaining the enemy's lies. What lies do you hear about yourself? List them, but not without replacing them afterward with the written Truth.

DAY THIRTY-TWO

UNCONSCIOUS FAITH

By faith the people passed through the Red Sea as on dry land; but
when the Egyptians tried to do so, they were drowned.
By faith the walls of Jericho fell, after the army had marched around
them for seven days.
By faith the prostitute Rahab, because she welcomed the spies, was
not killed with those who were disobedient.
Hebrews 11:29-31

Walking into something without any foresight or knowledge of what may come - having blind faith - is one thing. But what about partially blind faith? What about the times when we are aware of the people, the culture of an institution, or even the black-and-white facts involved in certain situations? A great measure of faith is certainly required to walk through such situations, but there is not a complete lack of sight or knowledge. I hadn't considered partially blind faith to be something - let alone something to consider stepping into - until today.

I saw a woman, not much larger than I, walking two dogs that - combined - easily weighed twice as much as she did. The fact that she was petite and walking two large dogs wasn't what led me to ponder partially blind faith; it was the fact that their leashes were connected to a strap she wore around her hips.

I used to run with my old boxer when I lived in Tucson. There was always something scurrying across the sidewalk – be it a tarantula or lizard, a distraction seemed to always present itself to her on every run. I would be in the zone, music in my ears, focused on the path before me when suddenly my entire body would jolt toward cacti and agaves because she saw something and therefore had to chase it. She was extremely well-trained, very disciplined, and great on a leash and off...but she was still a dog.

In order for that woman to walk her dogs the way she did, she had to have a great measure of faith in them and in herself. She also knew exactly what she was getting herself into when she buckled that strap around her hips and attached the snap hook to their collars. She had partially blind faith. She walked into something knowing full well it could be an absolute disaster, yet she had hope in the outcome and confidence in her preparedness, and she walked forth on the designated path bravely.

Partially blind, but still in faith.

I face many things with partially blind faith, often on a

daily basis. I think we all do. We enter our vehicles knowing the dangers that lie before us on the road, but we have faith that we will reach our destinations. We make career changes knowing the risk that uncharted territory brings, but we have faith that it will work out as it is intended. We walk in relationship with others knowing the risk vulnerability carries, but we pursue them nonetheless.

Our faith may be unconscious, it may be such an inherent thing that we don't give it a second thought, but it is there, right alongside our awareness of risk. Partially or completely blind, we live by faith.

DAILY REFLECTION

What are things you unconsciously put your faith in that actually pose great risk? What are things you walk regularly, or major life events you have endured, that have tested your faith? How is your faith similar in both instances? How is it different? Why do you think that is?

DAY THIRTY-THREE
ENEMY TERRITORY

Though an army encamp against me, my heart shall not fear;
though wars arise against me, yet I will be confident.
Psalm 27:3 (ESV)

The Lord brought something to mind today that occurred several years ago, back when I was still in that place of deep faith and trust. Some friends joined us in Detroit to pass out care packages to the homeless on the streets. A snag in our plan resulted in us bringing these items to a homeless shelter, which happened to be across the street from what seemed to be a gang house. Multiple men were posted on the front steps - in an arrangement that seemed strategic - wearing hostile, intimidating expressions.

After parking, I walked toward the homeless shelter to announce our arrival. Immediately, a man stepped away from his position on the porch of that house, crossed the street, and began walking toward me. I continued walking and when he was within just a couple of feet of me, I greeted him and asked how he was doing. He looked at me, hand clutching a gun under his shirt, and returned the greeting.

I am not a large woman by any means. I am just a little over five feet tall and not far past one hundred pounds. I am confident that I am not physically intimidating to anyone above the age of ten. Yet as I walked through what could be considered enemy territory, toward someone who had great potential to harm me physically, I had zero fear.

In the eyes of the world, what I did was senseless and irresponsible. Exiting a vehicle when an armed man - who came from a house with other armed men protecting it - walks toward you does appear senseless and irresponsible, until you consider what I was called to do. I was called to love and serve people, and there was nothing that could get in the way of me rising to that calling, not even what the world would deem to be a potentially dangerous situation.

The facts - my size, my gender, who surrounded us - didn't matter, because when you enter into enemy territory with the power of the Holy Spirit, everything is different. The same way I stepped into the mission He had for me that day, I have to step into the mission He has for me today, tomorrow, and all the tomorrows after - despite the seen and unseen dangers I may face.

DAILY REFLECTION

While most of us would regard a firearm in the hands of the wrong person as dangerous, there is also great danger in many unseen things. We can't necessarily see fear, anxiety, or depression, yet we know the danger they present to our health, our relationships, and our world. Sometimes the enemy puts us in danger in ways that are obvious to us – like what I faced that day. I would argue that most times, though, he is covert, disguising himself and his troops within the crevices of our daily lives and mission fields. As you reflect on your daily life and mission, where do you see the dangers the enemy has planted? Maybe it is physical dangers, like what I experienced, or maybe it is less tangible – unhealthy relationships, unresolved trauma, or temptation. How do you respond to them?

The facts - my size, my gender, who surrounded us - didn't matter, because when you enter into enemy territory with the power of the Holy Spirit, everything is different.

DAY THIRTY-FOUR
LIKE ELIJAH

Drip down, o Heavens, from above,
and let the clouds pour down righteousness;
Let the earth open up and salvation bear fruit,
and righteousness spring up with it.
I, the Lord, have created it.
Isaiah 45:8 (NASB 1995)

I don't think enemy territory always looks the same. In my experience, it looks vastly different than what we would expect both because it is where we walk daily and because the battle isn't always raging as we might think it would. At times, the battle is subtle, creeping slowly and covertly upon us until one day we realize that the enemy has closed in.

There is a beautiful pond in the woods where I find myself so often. Its borders typically remain a safe distance from the trail yet are close enough to beckon my attention. And beckon, they do, as a blanket of brilliantly green algae dances upon them and stretches across the vastness of the pond. It is simple yet fascinating and it brings me great joy to stop and take in its beauty.

On a recent hike, it caught my eye, but this time it was because it wore nothing. Its shoreline had receded due to a lack of rain in our fall season and, subsequently, the green evidence of its thriving health had diminished. While I stopped and took in the transformed sight, I knew that with each dry day that followed, the pond would become more nonexistent than the previous. It served as an example of that subtle, slow-creeping, covert type of battle, and it reminded me of the story of Elijah.

I tend to associate rain with God's mercies. Perhaps a subconscious way of finding praise in weather I do not find to be preferable, I always thank God for the rain. Yet during the three-year drought in the time of Elijah, God's mercy wasn't on hold. It wasn't locked in storage, waiting for the clouds to burst open so it could be released. Before the physical eyes of Elijah and of those who lived during that time, His mercy wasn't seen.

I wonder what I would have thought during the time of Elijah. I wonder if I would have been able to praise God for His mercy while my crops died, my family went thirsty, and we experienced suffering. I wonder if I would have been able to praise Him as the border of inherent hope seemed to recede. I know full well that His mercy isn't dependent upon weather patterns; we walk in a constant soaking of it. Yet, without the visual reminder, would I have even been able to see His mercy? Or would I have remained so focused on the perceived lack that I would linger in a place of immobility and inaction?

The truth is that I have no more control over what God does than that pond has over its filling or its drying up. I do, however, have control over my response. Like Elijah, I can accept God's provision in the drought, even if it is given in an unfamiliar manner. Like Elijah, I can remain in the midst of battle – be it raging or subtle and covert – and trust that at the perfect time, He will call me out. Like Elijah, I can walk into what He calls me to even if I don't know precisely what that is, as Elijah walked into God's calling of him with the widow. Like Elijah, I can face seemingly draining and bleak circumstances yet cling to hope that His brilliant blanket of mercy covers me even when it is not entirely obvious.

DAILY REFLECTION

How do you remind yourself of His presence, protection, and provision when He is not showing Himself obviously? Look for a few verses that you can memorize and speak out during those times, as a means of praising Him while simultaneously casting out the enemy, and write them below.

Like Elijah, I can accept
God's provision in the drought,
even if it is given in an unfamiliar
manner. Like Elijah, I can
remain in the midst of battle - be
it raging or subtle and covert -
and trust that at the perfect time,
He will call me out.

DAY THIRTY-FIVE
SELAH

Call to me and I will answer you, and will tell you great and hidden things that you have not known.
Jeremiah 33:3 (ESV)

I'm well-versed in seeking God with a mind full of clutter. I'll confess and say that for quite some time, that was the way I tried to seek Him. I walked away frustrated that He wasn't saying anything when the truth of the matter was that I didn't take my thoughts captive in order to hear Him. I leave no space for His Word when I am entertaining the words of the enemy, and while I would love to say I am completely beyond that, I am human and, on occasion, it happens...like today.

Clutter collided with my desire to hear Him this evening, yielding more frustration than what I was already experiencing because of the chaotic state of my mind.

Despite my attempts to surrender my thoughts, I continued in the push-and-pull of trying to quiet my them and then running with them into a state of full distraction. That is, until the whispering of one word: selah.

I know what this word means (to pause and consider what God has done), but knowing and understanding the meaning of something does not translate to effortless application. The application is unique to the circumstances, and as a person whose mind works incessantly, I often find myself to be the greatest obstacle between knowing and understanding something and applying that knowledge and understanding.

Progressively, the word selah's presence gained clarity, revealing what He had for me in it at this particular time. Each noisy thought was countered with the whispering of it, and with each utterance came an invitation to see how God wanted me to apply it. When it had fully developed, I found myself standing before the lone picnic table in the middle of my beloved woods. God asked me to literally live out the meaning of selah, which, in this instance, included lying atop that picnic table. I battled a small concern about what this may look like to those I had passed earlier on the trail. When they came upon a grown woman lying atop a wooden picnic table with her eyes closed in the middle of a state trail, what might they think?

I had to consciously choose to be willing, and my willingness was fueled by the frequency and prevalence of the word "selah" in recent days. I was quite aware that the clutter in my mind was due to my current season; a season of simultaneous waiting and wondering, hoping and praying, and trusting and surrendering. I had little choice but to live out its meaning. So, onto the table I climbed. The clutter dissipated. I was no longer wrestling with and battling my thoughts because I was living out the meaning of selah.

Transformed and prepared for whatever was to come, I climbed down and put my feet to the trail. I departed grateful for His calling of me on this hike, for the people and avenues through which He had gifted me that word in the days leading up to it, and for His flawless orchestration of an invitation to live out its meaning. I departed grateful for yet another measure of faith, as I was reminded that He speaks to us constantly - in the calm and the chaos - because of His love for us. Everything that happens around us all day contains His voice. His chosen medium and His message may vary, but His voice never does. And He is faithful to clear out the clutter with the uttering of even just one word:

Selah.

DAILY REFLECTION

Just as He repeated the word "selah" for me, God repeats Himself for all of us. What has He spoken on repeat for you? What is/was He inviting you into through that repetition?

DAY THIRTY-SIX
REMIND ME

The Lord is my Shepherd, I shall not be in want.
He makes me lie down in green pastures,
He leads me beside quiet waters,
He restores my soul.
He guides me along paths of righteousness for His name's sake.
Even though I walk through the valley of the shadow of death, I will fear no
evil, for you are with me;
Your rod and your staff, they comfort me.
You prepare a table before me in the presence of my enemies.
You anoint my head with oil; my cup overflows.
surely goodness and love will follow me all the days of my life,
and I will dwell in the house of the Lord forever.
Psalm 23

Psalm 23 is dear to my daughters and me. We memorized it during a season of drought as a means to shower ourselves with Truth. We recited it aloud nightly before bed and any time any of us was feeling anything but joy. I firmly believe speaking out Scripture is one of the greatest weapons we can have in our arsenal, and still recite Psalm 23 in the midst of struggle.

The words of this beloved psalm were deposited in my mind today. As the sun warmed my back, I was reminded that His goodness will follow me all the days of my life. I began to recite the psalm from the beginning and for the first time in the years its words have been ingrained in my heart, I noticed something: the first three verses are the psalmist talking about God, while the remaining three are the psalmist talking to God.

I don't know about you, but I feel completely different when I hear that someone has said something kind about me to another person than I do if that someone says the kind thing directly to me. There is something profoundly beautiful about receiving words of affirmation directly from someone as opposed to hearing them secondhand. There is a level of vulnerability that makes such an exchange more personal, more special, and more intimate.

I think we could agree that those who wrote the psalms did not necessarily struggle with being vulnerable with God, but I do wonder if Psalm 23 begins differently than it ends because of a lack of vulnerability. When I have allowed something to creep into the vulnerable space I share with my Jesus, it is more difficult for me to face Him. If I cannot face Him, I cannot speak to Him and I certainly cannot open my heart to Him. I have to remind myself of who He is before I am able to approach His throne.

Like he who penned Psalm 23, I have to speak out the Truth of who He is in order to have a properly postured heart. Only then can I praise Him for all of the beauty that He is, does, and will continue to do.

DAILY REFLECTION

Take a few moments to write about God as David did in Psalm 23. Who is God to you? What does He do for you? Do you call Him "Abba," "Jireh," "Raphah," "Adonai," "Ishi"? Why do you call Him this? Write until you sense He has released you. Do you notice the same progression in your writing (first you are writing about Him, then you are writing to Him) as in Psalm 23?

DAY THIRTY-SEVEN
FAITH PRECEDES THE PROMISE

Therefore, the promise comes by faith.
Romans 4:16a

A drawing my oldest daughter gave to me a few years ago stares at me from across my classroom every day from its place on the mini-fridge. It's a drawing of her, her sister, and me. We are outside during a rainstorm, they with umbrellas and I with a large rainbow on my head as if it were a hat. It found its way there about a week and a half ago, and I truly can't tell you why that happened. I stumbled across it and just felt like that's where it needed to go, so that's where it has been.

Like most parents, I receive drawings like this quite often. I don't save all of them. Typically, the ones I hold onto are the ones that speak to me, and, typically, the ones I keep in my field of vision are the ones God wants to use to speak to me in that particular season. Such is the case here. I have hung onto this drawing because of what she shared about it when she first gave it to me: we were in a rainstorm with umbrellas, but then a rainbow came and rested on my head. For good reason, God wants me to see this frequently throughout the day.

Storms always precede rainbows. That is to say, rainbows follow storms. I know that rainbows are a reminder of God's promise to never flood the earth again, but I believe they also are simply a reminder of God's faithfulness, which manifests through the completion of all of His promises.

In my experience, His promises are fulfilled after I participate. Created for relationship with Him, He invites me into His promises as a participant in their realization. Sometimes, that means I am to be still and trust. Other times, that means I am to rise to whatever occasion He has called me. No matter what the promise, how it comes to be fulfilled, or what my role is in its realization, there is one thing that is always true: His goodness - seen through His faithfulness in keeping His promises - follows me, because my faith, like the rains, precedes the promise seen in His rainbow.

DAILY REFLECTION

Are you in a storm or a rainbow season? How are you living out your faith within it? How have others spoken into your season or encouraged you in it?

DAY THIRTY-EIGHT
RIGHT WHERE HE LEFT IT

For you formed my inward parts; you knitted me together in my mother's womb. I praise you, for I am fearfully and wonderfully made. Wonderful are your works; my soul knows it full well.
Psalm 139:13-14 (ESV)

At some point or another, all of us have lost our phones, only to realize they're in our hand, or our sunglasses, only to realize they're propped atop our heads. It's funny because the place we find these things is always the place we last left them. Whenever it happens to me, it is because I have far too much going on around and/or within me to remember where I last left the very thing I need.

In the past eighteen hours, the very thing I needed was that rainbow promise, and there was simply far too much going on within me to remember where I had last left it. The external happenings of my day were nothing out of the ordinary, but they were too much when added to what I had going on inside of my heart and my mind. So much so that I knew my only choice was to abandon normalcy and seek until I found what I was missing.

What I was graced with in the abandonment of normalcy was amusing, actually, because it is something that is very much a part of my every day, both in its existence and in what came about this particular day: my hair.

The majority of my life was spent following trends. Like most females, I wanted to fit in, to be part of "that group." What that actually translated to was being lost and insecure; I either had no idea who I actually was or I didn't like who I was and wanted to hide...or, more accurately, both. It wasn't until just a couple of years ago that I was able to look the woman God created me to be in the eye and begin to embrace her. One of the ways this manifested externally was with my hair.

Seemingly superficial, our hair is actually in great part tied to who we are. We invest time and money into caring for and styling our hair, often employing it as a means of self-expression. This is reflected in what many cancer patients, especially women, report as one of the most difficult aspects of the treatment process. Our hair is a part of who we are. As such, denying myself the right - the privilege - to be who God created me to be for so many years resulted in denying myself from being that person even in the way I wore my hair.

On my venture to find what was missing, God reminded me that His promise was right where He last left it. His promise is woven into the unique identity He designed just for me. I wear that identity from the depths of my soul to the very tips of my thick, wavy hair, and when I am walking in it, people see, people notice, and people speak about it. Yesterday it was a quiet reminder through a sweet drawing. Today it was a loud, repetitive reminder through the kind words of absolute strangers.

DAILY REFLECTION

Do you think you are wonderful? I bet most of us would not answer that question affirmatively. We incessantly compare ourselves to others instead of saying the words of Psalm 139 in the mirror. I challenge you to speak the Truths of Psalm 139 while looking into your own eyes today. After, record what you felt. Which words stirred up emotions? What was hard to say? Do you see yourself differently now?

DAY THIRTY-NINE

RIGHT ON TIME

For the revelation awaits an appointed time; it speaks of the end and will not prove false. Though it linger, wait for it; it will certainly come and will not delay.
Habakkuk 2:3

I have a hypothesis about our birth stories. I detailed this on day seven, but in short, I was born eighteen days late. My poor mother watched as her due date, August 1, rolled past. Then a week, then another week, and then four more days. I decided it was finally time for everyone to meet me on August 19th, 1986.

I decided.

My life has centered around those two words more than it probably should. In fact, I wish I could say that I have grown out of the "I decided" nature I entered this world with, but I haven't. Over three-and-a-half decades later, I still do things on my own time, like embracing my identity or taking almost seventy days to complete this forty day writing task. Thankfully, God accounts for this in His plans. And thankfully, I am now in a place where I can accept His grace and forgiveness and see the goodness in His permissive will.

You see, if it weren't for my "I decided" nature, I would be writing this on September 9th, not November 12th. But if today were September 9th, God would not have been able to speak to me as He has; a great portion of what He has shown me has been through Creation. More specifically, He has spoken through autumn, which, in Michigan, begins long after September 9th. He knew I would veer off course and do this when I was ready to, and so He incorporated my "I decided" nature into His plans.

God's appointed time for things (for everything, really) has been a thought my mind has rested on frequently during the tail end of this journey. This wondering weaves itself with the concept of His sovereign and permissive will, and I am often left wondering how certain things would have played out if I (or whomever) would have simply cooperated the first time. I see this played out daily in the raising of my daughters; my preference is that they would cooperate the first time, but because of my love for them I allow them to choose. Sometimes, they choose wisely. Other times, they are like I was in the month of August thirty-six years ago, radiating stubbornness through the adherence to their own timelines.

While the latter is not my preference, the time between the first opportunity to cooperate and the time they finally do is extremely fruitful. In the midst of frustration, tears, and – at times – consequences, both my daughters and I are refined individually and within our relationships with one another. We grow in our communication and conflict resolution, we are bonded through acts of forgiveness, repentance, and reconciliation, and we are further molded into the people we were created to be. Though I cannot be certain, I think it is safe to say that His appointed time has nothing to do with time in the sense that we think it does. Rather, I think that God's appointed time has more to do with the ultimate desire of His heart: leading us back to the people He created us to be.

The only "I decided" that matters is the one that relates to deciding on Him; deciding to trust Him, to be led by Him, to be transformed by Him, to be loved by Him. We live out that "I decided" as restfully and comfortably as I lived out the eighteen extra days I spent in the womb, knowing that He has an appointed time for all things and He is refining us to walk into those things one "I decided" step at a time.

DAILY REFLECTION

You know how people say "it's easier said than done?" It's easy to say we have decided. What evidence is there that shows you have decided to trust Him, be led by Him, be transformed by Him, and be loved by Him? Write it out here, and if none exists, it will...because you will decide.

DAY FORTY

I DECIDED

*Trust in the Lord with all your heart and lean not on your own
understanding;
in all your ways submit to Him, and He will make your paths
straight.*
Proverbs 3:5-6

Normally there are seven days between my visits to the woods. In this fall season, that sometimes means I am introduced to a different forest weekly. Today's visit had just one day between it and the previous, which, combined with the fact that the trees are almost entirely bare, left the trail quite recognizable from the last time I had walked it. Yet, as I approached a fork in the path I began to feel lost and confused. I looked in the direction of where I knew I needed to go, but it didn't look right. After turning in a circle slowly, I checked the map on the post beside me, verifying that the direction I knew I needed to go in – the one that didn't look right – was, indeed, the path to take.

There have been many times in these woods (and outside of them) throughout these forty days when God has brought me to a place in my distant history. There have been other times when He has brought me to something that happened more recently. Even still, there have been times when He has enlightened me about something in my present that I was unaware of before. But this time, on this very last stretch of this forty-ish day journey, He spoke to me about my past, present, and future all at the same time.

Following a second confirmation that the map on the post wasn't lying to me, I took the unrecognizable path. As I advanced, things from the days of old came to mind, accompanied by amazement that beauty and growth were birthed in and through those trials. A chronological journey through some more recent life events and His work in and through them eventually led me to what I was walking that very day.

The unrecognizable path my feet were on served as a metaphor for the path my life was on. I knew I was in the right place - the place He wanted me to be. Just as He led me back to the trails today and told me which direction to walk, He had led me to where I was in my life and had given me ample confirmation of both what His desire for me was and what to do within it.

It didn't matter if what was before my eyes matched my interpretation of what He said; sometimes obedience looks different than we think it will or should. And while this time I had a trail map of sorts for where God was leading me in life, sometimes He doesn't provide that to me. As such, I have to trust Him – and whatever map He does give – even when the path I am led to looks as if it will bring me to a different place than He indicated it would. I have to make the decision to go forth knowing that the destination He is leading me to is His very best for me.

I decided. Today, I decided.

DAILY REFLECTION

At the conclusion of these forty days, I am put in mind of everyone in the Bible who walked a forty-something period. Like is true for me, I imagine both the path and the destination looked differently than they thought it would. Yet they continued forth, trusting in God with all of their hearts, submitting to Him, and leaning on Him - despite their imperfect and even rebellious moments.

Read about these Brothers and Sisters of ours: Noah in Genesis 7, the Israelites in Exodus 16, Moses in Exodus 24, Ruth and Naomi in the book of Ruth, or Jesus in Matthew 4. What can you glean from their experiences? Write it both here and on your heart as you walk into what God has been preparing for you on the other side of this healing journey: your Jubilee.

I have to trust Him - and whatever map He does give - even when the path I am led to looks as if it will bring me to a different place than He indicated it would.

www.ingramcontent.com/pod-product-compliance
Lightning Source LLC
Chambersburg PA
CBHW061822040426
42447CB00012B/2779